IRELAND

— ☘ —

FROM THE AIR

PETER SOMERVILLE-LARGE
PHOTOGRAPHY BY JASON HAWKES

Weidenfeld & Nicolson

London

CONTENTS

....

INTRODUCTION

....

SOME YEARS AGO I FLEW IN A MICROLIGHT FROM PORT PATRICK IN THE RHINNS OF GALLOWAY ACROSS THE IRISH SEA TO THE COAST OF ANTRIM IN NORTHERN IRELAND. FROM SCOTLAND I COULD SEE ACROSS THE WATER A SMOKING FACTORY CHIMNEY AND THE WHITE DOTS OF HOUSES SHINING IN THE SUN ON THE FAR SHORE. THE EASY PROXIMITY OF IRELAND TO THE LARGER BRITISH ISLAND, AN INVITATION TO THE INVADER, HAS CONTRIBUTED TO MUCH SAVAGE HISTORY.

COASTLINE AND THE CLIFFS OF MOHER, COUNTY CLARE

In geological terms the northwestern Clare plateau of upper Carboniferous strata consists primarily of coal measures with flagstones. The exposed flagstones reach the sea at the Cliffs of Moher, also known as the Wall of Thomond. There are five miles of these dark sandstone cliffs that menace the Atlantic.

People have been crossing the North Channel from Scotland to Ireland for more than 7,000 years.

The little engine hummed, and the wind caught our faces as we stuttered westwards in bright sunshine. In five minutes our view was transformed: the hills of Antrim vanished, and the coastline and the opening of Belfast Lough were screened in mist – Ireland might not have existed behind this blindfold. We flew on a little longer, hoping that this might be a temporary blip in the weather, but the ball of cloud grew denser and finally we gave up plans for penetrating a hidden country of darkened valleys and rugged mountains and retreated the way we had come.

I have also been fortunate enough to have seen Ireland's changing landscapes from the most intimate of aerial perspectives. In a hang-glider the pilot is free of insulation, with nothing between him and the wind but a harness to hold him above the hills and valleys, as well as the small moving fields. A hang-glider gives a hawk's-eye view: a few hundred feet up, suspended by fragile wings, the flier overlooks a landscape which takes on a unique perspective. The use of currents of wind and thermals with which to cover distance stresses the variety of the landscape beneath.

Any flight over Ireland offers the experience of a capricious climate which owes much of its fractious nature to its dominance by the sea. The island had 2,000 miles of coastline, and nowhere in the heart of the midlands is the sea further away than 70 miles away. The influence of channel currents and the sweep of the Atlantic is felt everywhere.

'The Irish air is Atlantic air,' wrote V. S. Pritchett, '. . .it is air empowered by the west wind, moist and rain-smelling, the lethargic air of heathery islands that are surrounded even more by air than by sea. One is excited and half asleep by turns.'

The history of aviation in Ireland has been linked to the sea from the moment in 1919 when Alcock and Brown were blown in by the Atlantic winds to crash on the Galway coast. Three years later, with the creation of the Free State, the Air Corps was founded, with the motto *Forfaire agus Tairiseacht* ('Alert and Loyal'). The Corps had in its possession eight Agro 504 Ks, eight Bristol fighters, four Martinsyde single-seater fighters and eight De Havilland 9A bombers, then the most modern available. In addition, there was the Martinsyde five-passenger plane which had been acquired by the Irish Republican Army during the Treaty negotiations, in case Michael Collins had to make an abrupt departure from London. It was christened *The Big Fella* in his honour.

In 1928, Commander James Fitzmaurice of the Air Corps took part in the first east–west crossing of the Atlantic. The fame for the Atlantic journey went to Lindbergh (who made the flight the other way in 1927), and Fitzmaurice remains a forgotten hero of aviation. Together with Captain R. R. MacIntosh, he first attempted to fly from Ireland to North America in 1927 in a Fokker monoplane, the *Princess Xenia*, but had to give up after flying 500 miles. The following year, he was a member of the crew of the *Bremen*, a Junker, which left Baldonnel Aerodrome at dawn on 12 April 1928. He was accompanied by two Germans: his co-pilot, Captain Kohl and the observer, Baron Von Heunfeld. They flew 2,300 miles in $36\frac{1}{2}$ hours before making a forced landing on Greenly Island off Newfoundland. They had accomplished a feat which was considered at the time 'the Everest of aviation'.

A decade later, the flying boats briefly brought passengers to Foynes, a few miles south of Limerick. Old men can still remember the elegant Sunderlands, known as 'Yankee Clippers', seeming like swans returning home, dipping their wings in the Shannon after their long flight across the Atlantic, before pulling up between the mainland and Foynes Island. The flying boats had their day between 1937 and 1945, before they were made obsolete by the opening of Shannon Airport, upriver at Rineanna, County Clare, to transatlantic aircraft.

The approach to Shannon from the west takes the aircraft past Loop Head, where the lighthouse rises defiantly from an almost submerged landscape: there is a glimpse of the great river before the plane crossed mud flats and brilliant green fields, and then the grey outline of a castle heralds the runway's approach.

The air approaches to Dublin, Belfast and Cork give a similar sensation of being swept in from the sea. Only at Knock is the link with the ocean severed. Here passengers from London or the bustling midland cities are deposited on *terra incognita*: a plateau rising out of a Mayo bog that is more substantial than the bog in Clifden that awaited Alcock and Brown. Jason Hawkes makes his view of a Ryanair jet parked on the runway at Knock a vivid study of sunshine and shadow.

It has been said that there is no such thing as climate in Ireland, but only an irregular sequence of weather patterns. The gales that sweep Ireland's western shores, the wind and rain, as well as the sudden gleam of sunshine catching a distant hill, are kaleidoscopic aspects of weather movement. It rains harder on the west coast, with the rain that Heinrich Böll described as 'absolute, magnificent and frightening', adding, 'to call this rain bad weather is as inappropriate as to call scorching sunshine fine weather'.

Rain can be seen as a means of uniting Ireland, although in his story, *The Dead*, James Joyce used snow to link east and west

'Ireland offers topographical variety in a tiny land area which is the result of an unusually complex geological history.'

in words that fall as softly as the flakes themselves. George Moore saw only gloom in 'blank snow-laden country, with its sepulchral mountains disappearing in the grey masses of cloud that the evening, like winding-sheets, slowly and silently unrolled'. Edith Somerville described the Twelve Pins in Connemara as 'elephants shrouded in muslin'. None of these authors, who were so affected by aspects of the weather, were contemplating aerial photography, however.

Giraldus Cambrensis was another writer who complained about the rain. In the twelfth century, he wrote that 'There is such a plentiful supply of rain . . . such an ever-present overhanging of clouds and fog that you will scarcely see even in summer consecutive days of really fine weather'. He may well have paid a visit to Ireland during a bad summer, for rain does not dominate. There is always a period when sunshine lights up landscapes, and when fleeting colours give different perspectives. In season, whitethorn gives way to gorse, hawthorn gives way to hedgerows of fuchsia and the mountain slopes are spotted with heather and western gorse.

Looking at Jason Hawkes' photographs, taken during a late-summer period, you would not believe that rain existed in Ireland. Instead, there is proof that, when viewed from the air, Ireland offers topographical variety in a tiny land area which is the result of an unusually complex geological history. An estimate of the oldest rock formations at Rosslare and Kilmore Quay in Wexford gives them an age of 2,000 million years. Granite, old red sandstone, metamorphic quartzite, fossil deposits, carboniferous shale, limestone and basalt all contribute to the make-up of the landscape. Among the most eye-catching examples of Ireland's geological development are the weathered outflows of cooled basalt that form the strangest of geological features, the truncated hexagonal columns of the Giant's Causeway.

Ireland has less tillage than other European countries; most of its farming land is still in pasture. From ancient times, since Queen Maeve set out to recover the big bull of Cooley, cattle have been a source of both wealth and contention. The rich pastures of the Golden Vale, the prosperous plains of Kildare and Meath, and the fertile farms of Kilkenny and Wexford have been moulded for thousands of years for the convenience of cattle.

Elsewhere, for centuries much of the country was dominated by bog – one-sixth of the Irish landmass was covered with raised or blanket bog. There are still stretches of land – like the area around Knock – which recall the description of Giraldus Cambrensis, who found Ireland 'uneven, mountainous, soft, woody, exposed to winds and so boggy that you might see the waters stagnating on the mountains'. The preservative powers of bog have resulted in clear botanical records, as ancient traces of birch, juniper, willow and other plants dating from before and after the ice age have yielded the secrets of the changing landscape.

Bogs contain hidden artefacts of many kinds: tools, bones, bog butter, bodies and treasure. The Irish elk, extinct for 10,000 years, has left its absurd horns deep in bogs like Ballybetagh outside Dublin. Chalices, crosses, torcs, and other treasures were concealed, lost and found in bogs. Some were only to vanish again, like the treasure in the Bog of Cullen in County Tipperary: between 1731 and 1774 regular finds, like 'a circular plate of beaten gold', 'a small gold crown' and 'a small gold cup' were sold off to goldsmiths to be melted down.

There are two kinds of bogs: the blanket bogs, which occur in rain-washed areas where the humidity is high, and the raised bogs of the lowlands, where badly drained stretches of flat plain have resulted in the peat accumulating to depths of 20 or 40 feet. It is on the raised bogs that machinery has moved in, at locations in Tullamore, west Mayo, or in the east Shannon basin, stripping away the turf and leaving a red desert. So thorough has been the work of mechanical cutters that the bog is becoming endangered.

The framework of south-west-tending Caledonian hills and east-west Armorican chains around which the lowlands are spread result in a land which is crossed by hills and mountain chains. Their names are beautiful: Slieve Bloom, Slievefelim Slievenamon ('the Hill of the Women') Ballyhoura, Galty Mor, Knockmealdown, Mourne, Sperrin, and so on. Generally the most dominant mountains are situated near the coast, resulting in the oft-quoted comparison of Ireland to a saucer.

In the west, the quartzite hills of Achill and Slieve League, as well as the ranges of Connemara, dominate the sea in Mayo and Donegal; a smaller, but equally impressive, cliff face is the Carboniferous mass in Clare which makes up the 600-foot-high Cliffs of Moher. The silver-quartz cone of Errigal in Donegal contrasts with the sharp ridges of the fretted outlines of Macgillycuddy's Reeks in Kerry. In the south-west corner, stretches of mountains split the inlets of Cork and Kerry like the fingers of a hand. In the east, the Mourne and Carlingford mountains are separated by Carlingford Lough. The Antrim hills reach down to Belfast Lough, a country which, in the words of John Hewitt is, 'groined by deep glens and walled along the west, by the bare hilltops and the tufted moors, this rim of arable that ends in foam'. In the south-east, the Blackstairs and the Comeraghs dominate Wexford and Waterford.

DUBLIN,
LOOKING SOUTH
During the 1970s and 1980s
property developers could
not wait to pull down the
shabby old heart of Georgian
Dublin, with its inconvenient
buildings that did not convert
easily into office blocks.

Like Belfast, Dublin has its own domestic mountains, which lead into the Wicklow Hills, part of the Leinster chain. When John Seymour described the sensation of glimpsing distant Irish mountains from Wales, regarding it as an invitation to make his home in Ireland, the range he saw was the Wicklow chain:

> What changed my life was that, over the bright blue brilliance
> that was the sea – and it merged with the sky so that there
> was no horizon – I could just discern a sight which stopped
> my very breath and seemed to turn my heart upside-down:
> hills, a range of hills, so faint as to be like a mirage, apparently
> hanging in the sky. It was so unexpected. I had looked over
> that sea a hundred times before and seen no hills. I gazed
> and gazed, for an hour perhaps, and if I was sober when
> I climbed the mountain I was drunk when I came down.

The majority of the Irish islands lie off the west and south-west coasts, sculpted by winds and Atlantic waves. The Skelligs, where hermit monks caught fish, developed their little plots of land and contemplated the trackless wastes of the sea, are the most spectacular. The inhabitants of the Blaskets endured hardship, as well as the lack of a harbour, until the 1950s; some of their people formed a chapter of Irish literature. The Aran Islands, with their stone paving and laced walls, great forts and memories of a rugged past, are harshly beautiful. In west Cork, the islands of Roaringwater Bay are scattered on the water like cards on a table. Most islands off Ireland are uninhabited now; most are situated less than five miles from the mainland, and none is more than ten miles away.

The country is threaded through by scores of brown and silver rivers and is divided by the complexities of the River Shannon and Lough Erne. Many rivers cross the midlands as slow-moving streams, often dropping and speeding up as they approach the sea. The Shannon itself is a sluggish stream before it fills the ice-hollowed basin of Lough Derg and begins its rapid descent: having dropped only 55 feet over more than 100 miles above Lough Derg, it falls more than 100 feet to the tidewater level at Limerick. From the air, you can see how it divides itself through Ireland. To the east, the three fluvial sisters, the Barrow, Nore and Suir, having flowed through the lush woodland and rich pasture of Kilkenny and Tipperary, join together in the bay that is Waterford harbour, before pouring into the sea. Other rivers cut eccentrically through mountain ranges: the curious course of the Liffey – partly submerged in the Blessington reservoir – that twists like a snake before bursting into Dublin Bay, follows an ancient, pre-glacial course.

Ireland not only has the longest river in the British Isles, the Shannon, but the largest lake, Lough Neagh. Lakes are scattered throughout the island, varying in form from Yeats' 'pools among the rushes that scarce could bathe a star' to the limestone complex of Carra, Corrib and Mask, and those – like Lough Erne or Lough Ree – which spread over soil with a high primary clay content. Many are corrie lakes which were gouged out during the ice age.

Although, in terms of geological time, the ice age took place only moments ago, glacial geology has moulded much of the landscape with which we are familiar. Successive ice sheets and glaciers moved far down the island; only parts of the extreme south and south-west escaped. As they moved and spread, they gouged out U-shaped valleys, moulded the backs of hills and mountains and formed rock screes, leaving scattered debris and evidence of erosion. Two legacies of the ice age in Ireland, drumlins, and eskers – ice-moulded ridges and accumulations of sand and gravel – have become part of an international vocabulary of geology. There is fossilized and geological evidence of extreme cold 10,000 years ago, probably resulting in permafrost. Such dominant and dramatic mountains as Errigal in County Donegal, and the limestone block of Ben Bulben in County Sligo were formed by glacial attrition.

Humans first arrived in Ireland very soon after the last ravages of the ice age, probably around 8,000 years ago. From the first they changed the landscape, cutting down forests and marking out field patterns that varied from rundale strips to the feudal systems introduced by the Normans, whose settlements tended to be in the fertile, bog-free, lowland areas of the south and east. Traces of man's past cover a wide time span, from the ring forts that are stamped on the hillsides to the Norman castle that is now used as a cattle byre and the furrows under the bracken that mark old potato beds. The planting of the Anglo-Irish has also left its impression on the landscape, although with the demise of the big house and its surrounding, landscaped parkland much has been destroyed.

Professor Frank Mitchell has written that in no other country in Western Europe 'are the corrugations of the surface representing activities of ancient man so clearly visible over large areas'. The agrarian nature of Irish society, with its emphasis on pasture, has preserved many ancient sites. Neolithic man left evidence of a stupendous civilization in the tombs on the north back of the Boyne, at Newgrange, Knowth and Dowth. Dolmens, tombs, monasteries like Clonmacnoise beside a bend on the Shannon, round towers (said to be Ireland's one contribution to architecture), Norman castles, headland forts and planter's mansions are all waiting to be viewed from the sky.

Today, in many places in the west, where badly drained land dominates, farmland gives way to forestry. Plantations spread up the slopes and summits of the mountains wherever the land is poor. The planting of coniferous trees is relatively recent: the oldest plantations, like Goughane Barra, date back only to the early 1920s – a few years after the founding of the Free State. Before the Sitka and Norwegian spruce took over, little more than one per cent of the countryside was covered with trees. Today, the trees that were planted as part of a deliberate, commercial policy make for an ugly but reliable

'Unlike the rest of Europe, where ancient cities and towns form the essential imprint of history, the traditional and romantic view of Ireland is a rural one.'

crop. Yet they are a poor substitute for the hard woods that suffered over the millennium, from the time that Neolithic man first ringbarked the oak to the depredations of the seventeenth-century planters. Before the time of the planters and their axes, however, much of Ireland's forests was already being destroyed by farmers, whose hostility to trees continues in some respect to this day. Forests are old enemies of pasture and tillage. An Irish rhyme runs:

Ireland was thrice beneath the ploughshare,
Thrice it was wooded, and thrice it was bare.

A few patches of the old forest survive: at Glengarriff in County Cork and in the Kerry mountains, the last haunt of the Irish red deer. These are places in which the monk once sought spiritual solace in his 'leafy desert'.

In a grey mantle from the top of bushes
The cuckoo sings:
Verily – may the Lord shield me –
Well do I write under the green wood.

No one could write well under a branch of Sitka.

Unlike the rest of Europe, where ancient cities and towns form the essential imprint of history, the traditional and romantic view of Ireland is a rural one. Too often urban centres were developed by invaders. The Celts were not town-builders – evidence of their civilization emphasizes elaborate monastic settlements and rural palaces. Traces of Clonmacnoise and Glendalough cover many acres. The spread of Tara – the most famous name in Ireland – whose origins are pre-Christian, is difficult to interpret from the surviving ruins. But these are not towns. We owe our major towns to the Vikings' judgment of good landing places. The little town they founded in Dublin Bay was taken over from a Celtic monastic site above the Liffey at Baile ath Cliath, the Hurdle Ford; at Cork they penetrated the massive harbour at Cobh and made their way upstream to a marshy patch beside the River Lee. Such little settlements developed into our main cities – Dublin, Cork, Waterford and Limerick were all Norse foundations. Galway evolved differently, after the Normans seized the lands of the O'Flaherty family, and Richard de Burgo built a stronghold on the site of a former O'Flaherty castle.

The variety of Irish landscape was slow to catch the camera's eye. The earliest surviving photographs of Irish scenes were taken by a pupil of Fox Talbot, the Reverend Calvert Jones, who travelled around Dublin and Wicklow in the early 1840s. Jones did not hesitate to include people in his pictures, in spite of the four-minute exposure time required in those days of early photography: although he preferred soldiers, who were used to standing still, his photograph of Trinity College features a bowler-hatted porter, while St George's Church, pictured in 1841, captures four gentlemen in stovepipe hats, as well as a blurred lady and a child.

Because equipment was expensive, photography was a natural pastime of the wealthy. The gentry soon took up the new invention, building their darkrooms in corners of their mansions. An early gentleman photographer, Strangman Davis Goff, of Horetown House in County Wexford, worked in the 1850s; his photographs are interesting, not only because of their age, but because he did not confine himself to his estate, instead roaming around Wexford taking scenes of the countryside on his wet plates. The Dillons of Clonbrock, a substantial Georgian house in east Galway, were enthusiastic recorders of hunting scenes, croquet parties, gardens, shoots, drawing rooms and every aspect of life in the big house. An endearing picture taken in 1899 shows five members of that Dillon family, each carrying a camera. Photography was considered a hobby especially suitable for ladies; the best were Lady Ross and the honourable Augusta Crofton, who produced records of children and life on their estates, or curiosities such as the great telescope of Birr.

News photography seems to have consisted largely of evictions, with the result that we have a clear idea of these dreadful scenes today. There are plenty of surviving photographic records of the barefoot children, religious processions, clachans, and shawled women of Connemara. Commercial photography first developed as records of popular places in the burgeoning tourist industry – the girls at Moll's Gap in Killarney, the Giant's Causeway, and other beauty spots, all offered subjects for visitors. The biggest collection of photographs of Ireland in the latter part of nineteenth century is a commercial collection. William Lawrence, who had a studio in O'Connell Street, employed a team of photographers (of whom the best known was Robert French, a former policeman), to circle Ireland with their cameras. The Lawrence Collection, now housed in the National Library, consists of 40,000 photographs of towns and tourist features, which fortunately escaped the fire that followed the 1916 rebellion. While Lawrence's stock of portraits were stored in Talbot Street and went up in flames, the postcard material was kept in Rathmines, out of harm's way. This was the material that French and his fellow photographers had recorded, and which included nearly every village main street in the country, big houses – many now gone to ruin – together with their cluttered drawing rooms.

Landscape photography came late to Ireland, perhaps because of the vagaries of weather. Aerial photography was pioneered in 1927, when the Ancients Monuments Advisory Committee for Northern Ireland commissioned the Royal Air Force to photograph archaeological sites such as Navan Fort and the Dorsey, an enclosure bound by earthen ramparts near Crossmaglen. Archaeology attracted other aerial surveys in the Republic, as the Irish Air Force recorded ancient sites, mostly prominent earthworks.

In the 1960s, a massive collection of aerial photographs relating to archaeology was compiled by the Committee of Aerial Photography for the University of Cambridge. The Cambridge survey, made before modern farming methods radically altered the landscape, was an invaluable record of Ireland's past. Pilots and photographers would use periods of ten days each July for reconnaissance and photography all over the island, accumulating 10,000 photographic records of raths, ancient field systems, cashels, early Christian sites, as well as crop marks revealing ancient structures that come into sight during hot weather. This record is in black and white, resulting in a technical rather than visual triumph. A wealth of new knowledge has been obtained by reconnaissance, which sought out sites and features that are invisible from the ground and were previously not known to have existed.

The Morgan collection, generated by Captain Alexander Morgan, DFC, consists of 3,000 sheet-film negatives of aerial views taken between 1954 and 1957. Although some were speculative, most were commissioned by clients, particularly newspapers. It is interesting to compare some of Morgan's black-and-white views with those taken over 40 years later by Jason Hawkes – Knock, for example, before the basilica was built, and the World Ploughing Championships of 1954, which comprises a study of parallel lines and patterns that has similarities with those seen by Hawkes' eye.

Various industrial surveys have been taken from the air, and various regional surveys deemed necessary for modern development. Brochures for factories and industrial estates are in demand as aerial maps. Other photographers provide aerial views for private clients, who will range from proprietors of hotels and golf courses to the proud owners of bungalows; a terrace of half-a-dozen houses photographed in the afternoon sun could easily provide five customers.

Such photographers, who generally do aerial sweeps every three or four years, are acutely aware of the changing nature of the ground beneath as the townscapes expand and the land succumbs to new buildings, changing farming patterns, afforestation and other agricultural methods. Modern intensive farming practices have resulted in green prairies, particularly in the east and midlands, where the soil is at its most fertile. Two hundred years ago, Arthur Young was struck by the naked look

There are few countries with more possibilities for the air photographer than Ireland, few countries whose colour and beauty is brighter, or at times almost overwhelming in its sheer splendour.

COASTLINE, COUNTY DONEGAL

The fact that so much of the coastline of Donegal is of cliff and rock is only one reason why such beauty is unspoilt. Another is distance – it is a long way to go for visitors. A third reason is the weather. My uncle, no friend of the tourist board, used to pray for rain each summer: 'Let it pour! Let it pour!' There were few things he liked better than the sight of dripping holiday makers in oilskins and macintoshes: 'They won't be back next year.'

of the Irish landscape, an appearance which is now returning as hedges and fences are pulled up. The bulldozer rampages, and the huge fields that result in its work that support the beef and dairy industries contribute to those famous 40 shades of green. A simple EC decision on subsidies for sheep has resulted in a transformation of mountain land, as the animals are now spread over mountains like lice, cropping the heather down to the black soil. Annually the towns and cities expand and bulge, the tentacles of new houses spreading outward. Roads appear to have acquired a new width by means of the bungalows strung out on either side.

Other aerial surveys are done by those in search of something more intangible, like the bird's eye seeking out beauty. One of the most successful of those who have photographed Ireland's landscape was Daphne Pochin-Mould, who flew over Ireland over 30 years ago, piloting her own small plane. She wrote: 'There are few countries with more possibilities for the air photographer than Ireland, few countries whose colour and beauty is brighter, or at times almost overwhelming in its sheer splendour. Set on the western seaboard of Europe this small offshore island is a place of mild moist winds, of a climate that varies not only from day to day, but from place to place on the same day.' Her photographs, in black and white, are fine examples of her skills in the vertical, or oblique, view, which are essential in looking at any chosen site. In general, the oblique, angled view of the countryside is more popular – and more artistic – than the vertical, which can often just be a form of mere aerial map-reading.

Today, the best aerial photography is done from a helicopter, as this book will testify. The helicopter's ability to move in any direction, to hover, to skip and jump wherever the pilot and photographer wish, make for a new interpretation of the scene below. The choice offered by the helicopter's slow and discriminating flight allows for a new artistry in the selection of subject.

In the early 1970s, I was flown by helicopter over one of the remotest stretches of Ireland: off the Sligo coast to the island of Inishmurray. The air of drama during that flight was emphasized by the presence of the guard at our takeoff on a lonely Sligo road to ensure that the machine was not snatched from us. In those days, helicopters were watched carefully, after the IRA had performed a couple of spectacular feats. We flew over the Ox mountains on a day when their western colours seemed to envelop us with their blues and greys. Why do Irish mountains seem bigger than their measurement in metres might suggest? Compared to those in Europe, they are pygmies, but in terms of effect they are majestic. Daphne Pochin-Mould

observed from her plane how 'these little hills can and do behave with all the savagery of high mountains . . . fierce winds can channel down the valley or sweep like surging waves over the mountains so that the air around is turbulent like mountain streams and updraught and downdraught can be so turbulent that the light plane's engine is unable to hold a level path through it'.

We flew out over a wrinkled sea (Tennyson used the adjective when he was in Ireland, in a poem about a Kerry eagle), to the small island of Inishmurray, with its cashel of stones and monastic enclosure founded by St Molaise. Now deserted, the small island has returned to wild solitude. As we hovered near the monastery, above a cloud of angry gulls, we could see clearly the patterns of old fields and stone walls that were sinking back into the gorse and heather.

Not everyone is fortunate enough to experience an epiphany like that. The next-best thing is to examine the aptly named Jason Hawkes' stunning photographs. Most aerial photographs eliminate the rough edges, the litter and the ruin, and turn the most wretched townscape into a miracle of symmetry. A few hundred feets' distance can disguise much ugliness: a pile of garbage vanishes into a dot, leaking sewage becomes a silvered river, a dump of rusted cars is transformed into a feature of the landscape. This does not mean that we have been deceived: the image from the sky is complementary to that on the ground, but is transformed by a formula of symmetry. Hawkes avoids the ugly bits, and it is his talented eye and his selection of the subjects that make these photographs exhilarating. From his Dublin townscape, where the bridges form a ladder over the Liffey, to his rock-climber's view of Ben Bulben, to his cows, boats, people, graveyard, big house, ruined castle, lakes, mountains and rivers – each subject, even the cows, is somehow turned into a work of art.

KENMARE RIVER, COUNTY KERRY
These views of pewter-coloured sea, sun and cloud near the Kenmare River confirm my belief that here is one of the most beautiful places in the world.

LEINSTER

The eastern seaboard of Leinster stretches southwards from the Ulster border at Greenore, taking in Dublin Bay, before reaching down to the tip of Wexford at Carnsore Point in Wexford. Westwards, a sandy coastline stretches to Waterford harbour. This is the long stretch of eastern and southern shoreline which has encouraged the stranger and invader, from St Patrick, to Strongbow, to Cromwell.

'*From the earliest times the province of Leinster has always been a place in which to settle and live.* '

The Vikings built their towns at Dublin, Wexford and Waterford, and established outposts at Arklow and Wicklow. Even the Romans, contrary to received opinion, made their way across the Irish Sea to the Leinster coast: there has been recent evidence that the Romans built a trading post north of Dublin at Rush. Leinster was Norman territory, and also the location of the Pale: based in Dublin, the Pale additionally encompassed coastal areas, while throughout the Middle Ages its inward boundaries fluctuated according to Norman and Gaelic fortunes.

Celtic Christianity has left its traces all over the province, in the form of early churches, round towers, high crosses, holy wells and such elaborate monastic settlements as Clonmacnoise, Glendalough and Fore. The Normans brought with them monastic settlers, whose sophisticated religious architecture – at its noblest in Leinster – include great Cistercian foundations like Mellifont, Bective, Tintern, Duiske and Jerpoint.

Leinster is by far the most densely populated of the four provinces of Ireland. The reason for this, of course, is Dublin, whose suburbs expanded relatively slowly until late this century. During the last 30 years, the capital has burst out into the neighbouring counties, which sometimes struggle to keep their own identity. The Wicklow hills limit further development to stretches along the coast that follow ancient roadways and passes, but the plains of Kildare and Meath invite urban growth. The setting of the capital is magnificent: punctuated by the outlines of the mountains, with the Big and Little Sugarloafs to the north, the snout of Howth Head at the southern end of the bay, and the Liffey bisecting a city that boasts a thousand years of turbulent history.

Here are a few names associated with Leinster: Oliver Goldsmith, Cuchulain, Swift, the Duke of Ormonde, St Kevin, Charles Stewart Parnell, Strongbow, John Synge, and Dermot MacMurragh. The saints and miracle-workers of Leinster are led by St Patrick, who lit the Pascal fire on the Hill of Slane. St Fintan's money tree is in County Laois, St Brigid's oak at Kildare, and St Mullin's well and perpetual ash tree in Kilkenny. Holy men sang of: 'Holly and hazel, elder and rowan and bright ash beside the ford.'

DUBLIN FROM THE WEST AND PHOENIX PARK
Dubliners can thank the Duke of Ormonde for one of the largest city parks in Europe, which covers 1,752 acres.

Ten other counties in the province provide landmarks that have moulded history, legend and religion. Let's take them one by one. There is Louth, the smallest and most northern county in Leinster, whose main town, Drogheda, is sadly well known on account of two Olivers: Cromwell and St Oliver Plunket, whose martyred head is preserved in St Peter's church. In Louth too are the most haunting of monastic sites, at Monasterboice and Mellifont. The Cooley peninsula, at the northern end of the county, which juts into Carlingford Lough below the Mourne Mountains, is the location of the most famous and bloodthirsty of sagas, the *Tain*, which describes the cattle raid of Cooley. The protagonists were Queen Maeve of Connacht, who coveted that wretched brown bull, and Cuchulain, who died lashed to a stone pillar at Clogfarmore, a raven resting on his lifeless shoulder.

Traditionally, Meath provided the richest pasture land in Ireland. Meath speaks of ancient kingdoms, of land that has been continuously farmed since the days of prehistory. Meath is where legend and ancient history shape the province, from tombs along the Boyne to the hills that are permeated with legend – Slane, Lloyd, Ward (which is associated with the Celtic god Lug), Loughcrew, which harbours its ghosts, and Tara, which made Meath Royal Meath. The Normans left their mark at Trim, on the banks of the Boyne, where the largest Anglo-Norman castle in Ireland, built by Hugh de Lacy in the earliest years of invasion, covers three acres. Meath was the setting for the last stand of Gaelic Ireland – also on the banks of the Boyne – and then for the long retreat of the exhausted soldiers, King James among them, over the bridge at Slane down towards Dublin.

Westmeath stretches westwards from Meath, out of the rich, drift-covered limestone into a wilder and poorer country with lakes – like Derrevaragh, where the children of Lir spent the last 300 years of their time as swans – down to the Shannon plain. Athlone, which guarded one of the most important crossings of the Shannon, was of strategic importance, and as a result was the site of numerous Celtic battles, as well as of an impressive Norman castle.

Longford reaches the eastern shores of the Shannon at Lough Ree, and shares some of the bleakness of Westmeath's scenery as well. Its capital awaits discovery, although perhaps it was unfair of Frank O'Connor to describe Longford town, the home of one of our Taoisai, as 'a terrible town'. One of County Longford's claims to civilized fame, Edgeworthstown, the home of the multitalented Edgeworth family, now goes largely unrecognized since its name was changed to Mostrim.

Kildare is associated with St Brigid, the patroness of

Ireland. In Kildare she is no substitute for a pagan goddess associated with fertility, but an identifiable personality: a young slave who took to the holy life in a way that impressed the King of Leinster. He presented her with a piece of land which is still known as Cill Dara, on which the oaken church where the saint established a nunnery in the late fifth or early sixth centuries is situated. She died in around 524, and the round tower that still stands in Kildare town must have been erected soon after her death.

On the edge of Kildare town The Curragh begins, a stretch of grassland which, in geological terms, is a sandy accumulation of morainic ridges. The largest area of arable land in the country, extending to 5,000 acres, The Curragh has always been a place for horses; on most mornings you can see horses exercising, and Ireland's richest race, the Irish Derby, is run here at the end of June. Elsewhere, Kildare is still a centre for horse-breeding, a place of guarded stud farms, white fences and distant Arab owners. The county's other famous racecourses include Punchestown, where a three-day steeplechase meeting takes place in April, and Fairyhouse, to which a foreign military presence made its way on Easter Monday, 1916, while a small group of fanatical amateur soldiers had other plans in Dublin.

Beyond Kildare is Laois (according to Betjeman: 'the hill-protected'), and also Offaly, counties which have the misfortune to be on the way to distant – let it not be said more interesting – destinations. If you doze off for a few minutes in Laois on your way towards Cork, you may miss it altogether. Offaly comprises an area of turf and bog on the way to Galway. These were lands once desirable to the English invader, who named them after King Philip and Queen Mary. They were patriotically renamed after Ireland became independent and King's County and Queen's County became Laois and Offaly respectively.

The central plain is a land of bogs. At Portarlington, or Allenwood, at Shannonbridge, the cooling towers where turf is compressed rise out of a leathery landscape that has been stripped by machinery. In Offaly there are more boggy areas than arable land.

Wicklow's hills guarded Dublin from the South, over the centuries they hid raiders and invaders. From the mountains the O'Tooles and O'Byrnes raided and burned the capital, and Strongbow and his knights slipped down by a pass above Rathfarnham. The hills, and the dark valleys and loughs among them, retain a feeling of melancholy and isolation that appealed to St Kevin, who brooded among the oaks at Glendalough (a few of them still remain). There is a stretch of oakwood at Coolattin, which the exertion of good men of the trees, headed

by Thomas Pakenham, has saved from the axe. Enough of Wicklow's landscape remains to earn its title 'the Garden of Ireland', but it is the mountains and their desolation that dominate. Augavannagh, Glenmalure, and Annamoe are Wicklow names evoked by John Synge, who wrote of 'the mists rolling down the bog', and the 'wind crying out in the bits of broken tree that were left from the great storm, and the streams roaring with rain'.

South of Wicklow Head is lowland, another fertile farming area extending through south Wicklow and Wexford. The Blackstairs, a dramatic mountain range never more than six miles in width, which extends for nearly 20 miles, stands between Leinster's two most prominent rivers: the Barrow, dividing Carlow and Kilkenny; and the Slaney, dominating Wexford. From Pembroke in Wales, the Normans sent over a small group of armour-plated knights to the south Wexford coast; at Beginbun, according to the rhyme, Ireland was lost and won. Hook peninsula is here, a bleak comma of land on which, observed Bishop Pococke, no trees grow. (He was wrong: there is one tree at least, leaning over in the wind beside Loftus Hall.) West of Hook, the little town called Crooke contributed to the legend that Strongbow said: 'I'll take Ireland by Hook or by Crooke.'

In County Kilkenny the medieval world survives in notable traces like the Cistercian abbeys of Jerpoint and Duiske, and the great castle that dominates the capital. This lovely county, with its trees, little hills, and the river valleys of the 'three sisters' – the Barrow, Nore and Suir – could be a setting for *The Canterbury Tales*. Carlow, squeezed out by the lush spectacle of Kilkenny, is another beautiful (and, inexplicably, one of the least-known) Irish county. In the eighteenth century, the Barrow brought prosperity to the towns along its banks; it joins the Grand Canal at Athy and, until recently, barge traffic made its way down to Waterford harbour.

Lugnaquilla, the highest mountain in the Wicklow range, shares with Tara a rural world that embraces the heart of Ireland. So does the great rock of Dunamace, the floating church of Mona Incha, Kilcooley Abbey, Ferns Castle and St Kevin's church and round tower at Glendalough. The Leinsterman is a blend of Celt and Norman and has 2,000 years of history behind him. Given its geographical prominence (facing across the sea to England), its moderate climate and rich pasture land, which is striped with fertile river valleys and mountain chains, from the earliest times the province of Leinster has always been a place in which to settle and live.

DUBLIN,

LOOKING SOUTH

Dublin prides itself on being well over a thousand years old. In 837 a group of Vikings, having decided that Dublin Bay was a good base for raiding, sailed up the Liffey, beached their long ships and founded a little settlement on the south bank of the river. The first cluster of wattle houses developed over the centuries beneath the Dublin mountains, the Liffey remaining its backbone. Louis MacNeice summed up the essential features of its turbulent history: 'Fort of the Dane, garrison of the Saxon, Augustan capital of a Gaelic nation.'

During the 1970s and 1980s property developers could not wait to pull down the shabby old heart of Georgian Dublin, with its inconvenient buildings that did not convert easily into office blocks. Many were associated with overcrowded slum tenements – in the bad old days, a large Georgian building could house a hundred people, twelve to a room. For two decades after the destruction of old Dublin, glass and concrete was substituted. Today, pseudo-Georgian terraces are being built all over the place, perhaps in the spirit of remorse. They are not as nice-looking as the old, departed houses, but are a lot more comfortable.

PHOENIX PARK MONUMENT, DUBLIN

The Wellington Testimonial, which is 60 metres high, was designed by Sir Robert Quirke, and paid for by public subscription as a gesture of thanks to the Iron Duke. Nelson's Column, the other oversized monument to an imperial hero, was blown up in 1966 to mark the fiftieth anniversary of the Rising. However, Wellington's memorial has so far escaped the consequences of statue politics, although it is doubtful if its bulk could withstand Semtex. As far as I know, no one ever took an aerial photograph of the Admiral on his plinth. Wellington was Irish born (in Merrion Street in Dublin), but his exploits were in England's name.

THE FOUR COURTS, DUBLIN

Upstream from the Custom House on a bend of the river, James Gandon built the Four Courts, incorporating and enlarging on a design of Thomas Cooley. The interior of the copper dome with its double skin, was inspired by the Pantheon. This interior was destroyed during the bombardment of the civil war of 1922. More disastrous was the loss of the Public Record Office next door. In the explosion, registrations of births, marriages and deaths, census returns, the records of the High Courts, and other documents relating to the whole of Ireland were scattered all over Dublin. The loss of a nation's parish records is hard on those emigrants who return and search for evidence of their ancestors: they find that their great-grandparents' birth certificates ended up as pieces of ash in suburban back gardens.

CUSTOM HOUSE, DUBLIN

James Gandon, whose architecture transformed Dublin, arrived in Dublin from England in 1781. He was beset with difficulties in building his masterpiece, the Custom House: there was fierce hostility from Dublin's citizens, and the site was on reclaimed slob. The work took ten years, at the enormous cost of £400,000. Over a century later the building was reduced to a shell during the Troubles and rebuilt. Gandon would not recognize the interior, but the exterior remains handsome, particularly since its recent embellishment. Jason Hawkes is flying too high to catch the decorations on its façade: the lions and unicorns, heads of oxen, and river masks.

**CUSTOM HOUSE,
LOOKING WEST UP THE
LIFFEY, DUBLIN**

On the right of the Custom
House is the tower of Liberty
Hall, which contrasts
flippantly with Gandon's
dome. The original Liberty
Hall on Eden Quay, the
headquarters of James Larkin
and the Irish Transport and
General Worker's Union was
declared 'unsafe' in 1958. The
heroic old building was
therefore demolished in the
name of progress and replaced
by the new Liberty Hall, with
its frivolous green canopy.

**TRINITY COLLEGE,
DUBLIN**

Nothing remains of the
original Trinity College,
which was begun in 1591.
The chapel, buttery, kitchen,
hall and main square court,
paved with thin, red Dutch
bricks have vanished, and most
of the buildings used today
date from the eighteenth or
nineteenth century. The New
Library, however, designed by
Paul Koralek is perhaps one of
the finest examples of
twentieth-century architecture
in Ireland.

HALFPENNY BRIDGE, DUBLIN

The graceful footbridge beside Wellington Quay is known as the 'Metal Bridge', from the iron of which it is made, or the Halfpenny Bridge from the toll it once charged. In 1816 Alderman Beresford and Mr William Walsh paid £3,000 to have it built, to replace a ferry. The city got its money back in halfpennies. It is no longer a toll bridge, but today there are two modern toll bridges over the Liffey which charge considerably more than a halfpenny for every car that crosses them.

GUINNESS'S BREWERY, DUBLIN

Guinness has occupied the site of St James' Gate since 1759, when Arthur Guinness purchased Rainford's Brewery. It is not so long since barges used to go down the Liffey carrying barrels of stout to waiting ships in the bay. They used to dip their funnels as they went under the bridges. My father remembered standing on Capel Street Bridge, beside a Dubliner who yelled down to a steersman: 'Bring us back a monkey or a parrot!' At one time the brewery had a little railway. Today, if you visit the complex, you can study an audiovisual account of how to manufacture the famous pint, and, better still, they give you a glass of Guinness for free. (There's no Liffey water in it.)

ROYAL HOSPITAL, KILMAINHAM

The Royal Hospital, which is older than the similar hospital in Chelsea, was begun in 1680, to the design of the Surveyor General, Sir William Robinson. It had been commissioned by the Lord Lieutenant, the Duke of Ormonde, who had seen the *Invalides* in Paris during his exile in France. Until 1922 it housed 'ancient maimed and infirm officers and soldiers'. In the following decades, its premises were used to store unwanted exhibits from the National Museum, as well as the bronze statue of Queen Victoria, known as 'England's Revenge' on account of its ugliness. (The queen, who was removed from the front of Leinster House in 1948, has now gone to Sydney.)

The hospital with its chapel and courtyard surrounded by a covered loggia, and the tower, which once had a bell known as the 'Old Cow of Kilmainham', gradually decayed. Then, in the 1980s, a fairy godmother appeared in the form of the European Structural Funds. Restored at a cost of £20 million, the Royal Hospital is now designated a National Centre for Culture and the Arts.

O'CONNELL STREET, DUBLIN

The triangle at the bottom of this photograph is a stretch of the Liffey. Beside it is O'Connell Bridge, once Carlisle Bridge, which was completed in the 1790s, just in time for the rebels of the 1798 rebellion to be hanged from the scaffolding that covered it. In 1880, the bridge was widened to take the increasing traffic, which included the new, horse-drawn trams with knife-board seats on top. It was then renamed O'Connell Bridge Although the street to the north of the bridge officially kept the name Sackville Street (after Lionel Sackville, Duke of Dorset), for many years afterwards, Dubliners knew it as O'Connell Street. 'It is useless', commented a traveller in 1892, 'to speak of it to your driver by any other name . . . he will pretend not to understand you.' To emphasize the name, the O'Connell monument was erected to the design of John Henry Foley. If you were viewing the monument from the ground, you would see bullet holes in the winged figures of Patriotism, Fidelity, Eloquence and Courage, as well as Eire released from her chains – which the ladies received either during the insurrection of 1916 or the civil war in 1922.

DUBLIN CASTLE

In 1204 King John of England ordered the building of 'a castle . . . for the use of justice in the city . . . with good dykes and strong walls'. For centuries 'the Devil's half-acre' not only provided an official residence for lords deputies and lords lieutenants, but also defended the city. Between 1680 and 1780 the castle was transformed and embellished with Georgian buildings. This view looks down on the Upper Yard which covers more or less the layout of the medieval fortress. The tower of the Castle Hall is flanked by two arches with statues of Fortitude and Justice. The dome in the foreground belongs to the City Hall.

DUBLIN CASTLE

This view of the Lower Yard shows the Record Tower, now the State Paper Office, which was given a Gothic embellishment by Francis Johnston in 1811, and the Chapel Royal in the 'Gothick' style, also the work of this most romantic of Irish architects.

DUBLIN FROM THE WEST AND PHOENIX PARK

The western approaches to Dublin never became residential, partly because of industrial development beside the Liffey, and partly because of Phoenix Park. Dubliners can thank the Duke of Ormonde for one of the largest city parks in Europe, which covers 1,752 acres. After the Restoration, the land, which was once owned by the Knights Hospitallers, reverted to Charles II who was tempted to give much of it to one of his mistresses to use as a deer park, until Ormonde dissuaded him from this plan. There are still herds of deer in the park.

THE DUBLIN TO HOLYHEAD FERRY
Much the best way of viewing the Holyhead boat is from the air. At sea level, it looks like a giant shoebox, its designers having sacrificed grace for parking space. This ferry takes three hours to cross the Irish Sea; there are faster vessels, which cross in an hour. In the days of sail, the journey could take days, and passengers had a good chance of being seasick (like Oliver Cromwell or John Wesley), drowned, or captured by pirates.

**GOREY,
COUNTY WEXFORD**

Gorey is a busy market town
on the east coast a few miles
inland from the sea whose
main street is also a stretch of
the highway between Dublin
and Rosslare. I suspect from
the shadows and the small
amount of traffic that Jason
Hawkes' helicopter hovered
late on a summer's evening.

CEMETERY, GOREY, COUNTY WEXFORD

The departed rest easy beneath a grey patchwork, among crosses and spreads of green-marble chips. A latecomer has flowers above him. Gorey churchyard is a traditional burial place for itinerant families, as many of the elaborate headstones testify.

CARAVAN PARK, COURTOWN, COUNTY WEXFORD

From the air the caravan park, divided by two roads, falls into a neat pattern.

**ARKLOW,
COUNTY WICKLOW**

The handsome church at the
top of Arklow's main street
was built in 1840, the work
of Patrick Byrne, a popular
ecclesiastical architect, who
was also responsible for
several churches in Dublin. In
the early nineteenth century,
a good number of huge
Catholic churches were
designed in this heavy,
classical style; they were
meant to evoke the spirit of
Rome, both imperial
and papal.

**ARKLOW,
COUNTY WICKLOW**

Arklow was a Norse
foundation, which in
Norman times, became a
Butler stronghold. It has
always been a busy seaport; in
the nineteenth century,
coasters anchored here to take
copper and lead from the
mines in the Avoca valley
over to Swansea to be
smelted. One result of its
long-established boat-building
tradition is the training ship,
The Asgard, a 28-ton white
yacht which was used to
bring 900 rifles and 29,000
rounds of ammunition from
Hamburg to Howth in 1914.

WICKLOW TOWN

My family had a bookshop in Wicklow for a short time. It was not successful; the most popular books were novels by Danielle Steele and treatises on arthritis. However, the experience gave us a fondness for the sturdy little seaport, with its nineteenth-century houses, eighteenth-century gaol, monument to Billy Byrne, and obelisk commemorating a local son, Robert Halpin, captain of the *Great Eastern*. A narrow creek runs through the town, which receives the waters of the River Vartry.

**LIGHTHOUSE,
WICKLOW HEAD,
COUNTY WICKLOW**

There is the ruin of a castle near here called Black Castle, which was built by the Normans. But the Vikings were here before them: they founded a settlement called Vikingalo, or Viking Lough, and would have posted a sentry or burnt a furnace here on Wicklow Head to help guide their longships. Like all the rest, this head lighthouse is now automatic, and there are computers to keep the light moving, instead of keepers who amused themselves by putting ships in bottles.

COASTLINE SOUTH OF ARKLOW, COUNTY WICKLOW
Sandy beaches, protected by undulating dunes south of Arklow Head, roll down towards Courtown. Arklow itself is an ancient seaport, founded by Norsemen around the tenth century.

Some time before, St Patrick is supposed to have landed in this area, according to one of hundreds of legends concerning the patron.

BRITTAS BAY AND SILVER STRAND, COUNTY WICKLOW

Brittas Bay (above) and Silver Strand (left), south of Wicklow town, are the first decent sandy beaches to the south of Dublin. To the north, the seaside stretch between Greystones and Wicklow is of pebbles and grit. As a result, thousands of Dubliners make for these more southern beaches during summer weekends, and a good sample is to be seen in these pictures.

Silver Strand has to be reached by descending a steep path down the cliff. You find yourself enclosed by cliffs and with the tide coming in. This picture was taken in the afternoon, when the sun has a tendency to depart, leaving shadows behind.

LITTLE SUGARLOAF, COUNTY WICKLOW

You have to view the Little Sugarloaf (above) from the north, where you cannot see its long, undulating back, in order to get the same Mount Fuji effect.

**FIRE ON THE BIG
SUGARLOAF,
COUNTY WICKLOW**
The Big Sugarloaf, a quartzite
peak 1,659 feet high, has the
look of a volcano, which, in
these pictures, is enhanced by
the fire on its slopes.

Harvesting, ten miles south of Dublin

At first, harvesting was done with sickle and scythe. In parts of the country, a distinctive bow was added to the scythe when reaping corn, in order to leave it in bundles ready for tying in sheaves. Scythes were replaced by reapers and binders and the threshing machines that lingered into the 1960s before the advent of the combine harvester, whose neat work is visible here.

TURF CUTTING, COUNTY OFFALY

In the sixteenth century, John Derricke wrote of 'a shakyng bogge, a fort of passying strength, from where a certain fire is drawne to sheeld from winter's cold'. In those days, bogs were everywhere. The 'horrid wilderness' is now exploited by machines which Austin Clarke described as 'saurian'. They strip the turf from the ground, leaving a red desert. This natural resource, which, for centuries, gave warmth to the fireside, is used mainly in turf-burning power stations, or the turf is compressed into briquettes for domestic use. In a decade or two, it will be exhausted.

THE CURRAGH, COUNTY KILDARE

There are over 5,000 acres of The Curragh, the largest area of arable land in the country: 'a more beautiful lawn than the hand of art has ever made', according to a nineteenth-century traveller. It is devoted to sheep, soldiers and horses.

Thirty years ago, the racecourse was unfenced, and the horses appeared to gallop over an empty plain on The Curragh's peculiarly springy turf. Nowadays, the stands and fencing offer the best in racing, and the Irish Derby takes place in more sophisticated surroundings.

THE GRAND CANAL, COUNTY KILDARE

The Grand Canal cuts Kildare in two at an early stage in its path westwards towards Shannon Harbour and Ballinasloe. Passenger travel on the Grand Canal was inaugurated on 9 June 1788. The Royal Canal came later. Packet-boat travel flourished for half a century, providing first- and second-class accommodation for affluent travellers. Those who chose second class had to sit on the open cabin roof and duck whenever they came to a bridge. 'Fly' passage boats were the fastest; four horses, exchanged frequently, took them along at a gallop at, an average of eight miles an hour.

Anthony Trollope was one passenger on these boats; although he presumably went first class, he loathed the experience. The 'misery' included tedium, discomfort, and being supplied with 'the eternal half-boiled leg of mutton floating in a bloody sea of grease and gravy' and 'vast heaps of yellow turnips'. However, it was not the catering but the railways that destroyed the traffic on the Grand Canal.

TURF CUTTING, COUNTY KILDARE

Bog air was believed to be healthy. In 1802 the Reverend Sharkey, a native of Roscommon, wrote: 'Our having remained so long free from plagues might be attributed to the antiseptic and astringent nature of our bogs and marshes, whose exhalations must also be of that disposition'. Plenty of people, including the Duke of Wellington, have had ideas of draining 'the bogs and morasses of Ireland' and turning them into pasture. One eccentric, Richard Pockrich, an eighteenth-century millionaire, wanted to plant them with vineyards or, failing that, bamboo.

ST PATRICK'S COLLEGE, MAYNOOTH, COUNTY KILDARE

St Patrick's College, Maynooth, was founded in 1795, after the British authorities had become worried that Irish priests were picking up revolutionary ideas in the Continental seminaries to which the Penal Laws had forced them. Now they could train at home. In the words of George Bernard Shaw, 'the young priests of Ireland are taught that if the world is not exactly flat, it is not quite so round as it is generally supposed to be'.

The architecture of the building is a mishmash of nineteenth-century triumphalism. Pugin had a hand in it, and the tower of the College Chapel that you can see in the photograph is the work of J. J. McCarthy, who was known as the 'Irish Pugin'. Pope John Paul II landed in one of the two great quadrangles during his visit to Ireland in October, 1979. The largest Catholic seminary in these islands, St Patrick's is also a university, which has admitted women for the last two decades.

MUNSTER

·················

The variety of Munster's
scenery, ranging from the flat
lands in Limerick and the low-
lying plain beside the Shannon
estuary, the harsh terraces of
the Burren in County Clare
to Tipperary's Golden Vale,
mirrors in miniature the
variety of Ireland's
countryside in general.

THE BURREN COASTLINE, COUNTY CLARE

From afar, the limestone which makes up the Burren looks like snow. Near to, it swirls around mountains like Black Head and Mullagh Mór, or lies flat on the ground, split up into little ravines called grykes, filled with ferns. The stones ring out when you walk over them. It is a country of portal tombs, ring forts and suspicious farmers. The alpine-arctic flora of the Burren bring botanists, especially in spring. This stretch of coast (below) is at Black Head. When I was last at Black Head, the gentians were growing like buttercups elsewhere.

MUNSTER

·············

THE VARIETY OF MUNSTER'S
SCENERY, RANGING FROM THE FLAT
LANDS IN LIMERICK AND THE LOW-
LYING PLAIN BESIDE THE SHANNON
ESTUARY, THE HARSH TERRACES OF
THE BURREN IN COUNTY CLARE
TO TIPPERARY'S GOLDEN VALE,
MIRRORS IN MINIATURE THE
VARIETY OF IRELAND'S
COUNTRYSIDE IN GENERAL.

In Munster there are also the mountains; from the air they show themselves in a unique fashion: the pilot can look down into corries and valleys from a perspective that no climber can, seeing their walls and the lakes tucked into their folds in a way that suggests arrogance, omnipotence and divinity. Munster is dominated by the east-west mountain ranges, the Comeraghs, the Galtees, the Knockmealdowns and other lines of hills that extend from Waterford westwards into the peninsulas of Kerry and Cork. A knot of wild mountains centres on Killarney, dominated by Macgillycuddy's Reeks, including Carrantuohill, the highest peak in Ireland, and the startling Paps, unsurprisingly associated with fertility and the Celtic attractions of the goddess Anu. Other, solitary mountains invite legend: Slievenamon in Tipperary, and Knockshigowna – both homes for the fairies – while Ardpatrick, Ireland's highest green hill, caused St Patrick to found a monastery there.

The eastern point of Munster's coast is at Waterford city, whose quays adjoin three mingled rivers: the Nore, Barrow and Suir. Waterford was one of the most important of Anglo-Irish foundations on the eastern seaboard. Reginald's Tower, cylindrical and massive, is a pointer to the Norman past, but much of the rest of this little county town is provincial Georgian in architectural style. To the west the coastline contains, in addition to strident seaside towns like Tramore and Dungarvan, a string of tiny villages, attended by stretches of strand: Ardmore, Stradbally, Bunbeg and Bunmahon, where folk from the hinterland for centuries took their holidays.

At Bunmahon, Dorothea Herbert came for 'Sea bathing' in 1791, travelling from Carrick-on-Suir 'on Common Cars with our Beds and Luggage', to stay in 'a set of dirty Cabins newly White wash'd indeed, but quite destitute of Elegance – as they served in the Winter for Cowhouses and Pig Styes'. The little strand, backed by the Comeraghs, once a haunt of the outlaw, William Crotty, is still almost as wild as she found it.

The intermittent beaches of Waterford and east Cork give way to one of the world's most spectacular harbours. The entrance to Cork harbour at Cobh is a mile-wide gap through a ridge of old red sandstone, behind which is the submerged valley which forms extensive anchorages and deep channels for shipping. Cobh is associated in Irish minds with the flight from the land following the famine. From here the dispossessed fled in their millions to the New World. Outside the dramatic entrance to the harbour were anchored the old Cunard and White Star liners. On these empresses of the sea passengers sailed along the coast, past the Fastnet Rock (nicknamed 'the Teardrop of Ireland'), seeking a better life, and never to return. Today those who leave for America go to another province,

and fly off from Dublin or Shannon, leaving the old sea passage a fading memory. However, much of the atmosphere of departure and emigration has been wonderfully preserved in the Cobh Maritime museum, where you can sail in a coffin ship, grow seasick on the Atlantic crossing, and board *The Titanic*.

West of Cork city, Kinsale and the little coastal towns of west Cork attract visitors and strangers, many from England. Many stay, although it is hardly fair to say that, as I overheard in Skibbereen, west Cork has become like Tunbridge Wells. The fretted coastline attracts yachtsmen from England and France, while Schull and Baltimore, situated on Roaringwater Bay among Carbury's Hundred Isles, are within driving distance for the Volvos that set out for Rosslare. There are those that settle in farmhouses overlooking Horse Island, the Three Calves, Cape Clear, Sherkin and the rest. The transition is not always successful, and there have been too many five-year cycles of failed experiments. First year: farmhouse bought on a sunny day. Second year: conversion, decoration. Third year: boredom, drink problem. Fourth year: divorce. Fifth year: departure. But in recent years these cycles of despair seem to be getting longer. Perhaps the fax machines and telephones keep the newcomers in touch with England and the Continent. Perhaps the weather is getting better. Perhaps the Gulf Stream is as warm as they make out.

The Cork and Kerry fiords can be reached by yachtsmen. It is a pleasant occupation to stand at Mizen Head, the most southwesterly corner of the British Isles, and watch the little yachts claw their way round it. The rolling ship may make its way round into Bantry Bay, and through Dursey Sound into the spectacular Kenmare River. Kerry is where the Gulf Stream really does its work: under the bare hills the protected southwestern inlets present a natural luxuriance that is derived from their geographical advantage and their relation to the famous Gulf Stream. There is little or no frost, and only occasionally a sprinkling of snow. Gardens like Derreen or Garinish happily support palm trees, tree ferns and the other tropical plants that believe that they have discovered a monsoon – or perhaps an eternal spring. The winter mean temperatures of 44°F in Kerry and west Cork are similar to those of Biarritz and Marseilles, but the rain in winter can be ceaseless: on the coast between Sneem and Cahirciveen, three-fifths of Ireland's mean annual rainfall of 56 inches falls between October and March, with rain on three days out of four.

The fertile quality of Munster is reflected on the mountain slopes above Killarney and around Glengarriff, where the last of the oak forests survive and even flourish. By contrast, at the Burren (*boirinn* – stony place), on the limestone, which is splashed in season with brilliant blue gentians, saxifrage and orchids, and where Mullagh Mór is shaped like the Tower of Babel, forest did not grow. Apart from the hazel thickets, there is not a tree on which to hang a man.

The coastline north of Tralee is halted by the Shannon estuary; here Munster faces Connacht on the east side of the river, which veers north-east past Ardnacrusha power station towards Limerick city. Its Leinster route will take it upstream to Athlone and Lough Derg. But the Shannon, bulging with lakes and shared by Connacht, is a water highway that does not inspire the same affection that Munster's own rivers do. The Suir, Blackwater and Lee not only share a common Munster background, but also the same self-willed disposition suddenly to change course from east to south. The Lee, which turns southward below Cork city, rises in St Finbar's black lake at Goughane Barra before flowing through the mountainous land at the heart of County Cork. The Blackwater, whose wooded and castellated valley has been over-enthusiastically compared to that of the Rhine, turns at an angle of 90°.

The number of Munster's abbeys, castles and other antiquities is almost as great as that of its golden fields. Take them by age, from the ring forts, stone circles and cashels, to the minute Gallarus Oratory on the Dingle peninsula that resembles an upturned stone boat, to the solitary towers on west Cork's coast, while the Rock of Cashel, a perpetually unexpected surprise and delight to the traveller, offers the perfection of Cormac's Chapel. But Jason Hawkes' travels through Munster concentrate less on these celebrated landmarks, and more on the exploration of light, shadow and pattern, or the way in which water, like the Lee in Cork or the sea's edge at Kinsale, snakes its way through the towns' buildings.

'I walked all over Munster mild' ('an Mhumhain mhín'), wrote the poet, Aogan O'Rathaille, grieving for the loss of the old Gaelic lords, with their traditions of hospitality. Hawkes has covered Munster mild, the 9,536 square miles from Doire corner to Dun na Ri, in a happier spirit. It is a long way from Tipperary, the only landlocked county in the province, to the outermost islands on the south-west coast.

COASTLINE AND THE
CLIFFS OF MOHER,
COUNTY CLARE
The highest point of the cliffs is at the northern end, where they rise to 668 feet. The camera, of course is much higher, looking down on sea foam. During westerly gales, the wind carries the sea spray right up the cliff face and over the edge.

SIGNAL TOWER, CLIFFS OF MOHER, COUNTY CLARE

This signal tower is another abandoned tower at Hag's Head, at the southern end of the cliffs, which are a comparatively modest 407 feet high. At the more dramatic northern end is O'Brien's Tower, a disused tea house built in the last century by Cornelius O'Brien, MP, for the convenience of visitors. Mr O'Brien also built a monument to himself at nearby Birchfield House: a masonry column topped by a lopsided urn which bears a description of his virtues. He has never been forgiven for making his tenants pay for it.

BUNRATTY CASTLE, COUNTY CLARE

There has been some sort of fortress guarding the ford beside the little Ratty River for 700 years. But it was Donogh O'Brien, the fourth Earl of Thomond, who made Bunratty Castle his seat, enlarging the keep and building the turret. William Penn's father had it for a time. It became a ruin and remained so until 1954, when it was purchased and restored by Lord Gort, in a brilliant recreation of the massive proportions of the O'Brien stronghold. Now it is a magnet for tourists, the location for smoothly organized, and enduringly popular medieval banquets.

THE BURREN COASTLINE, COUNTY CLARE

From afar, the limestone which makes up the Burren looks like snow. Near to, it swirls around mountains like Black Head and Mullagh Mór, or lies flat on the ground, split up into little ravines called grykes, filled with ferns. The stones ring out when you walk over them. It is a country of portal tombs, ring forts and suspicious farmers. The alpine-arctic flora of the Burren bring botanists, especially in spring. This stretch of coast (below) is at Black Head. When I was last at Black Head, the gentians were growing like buttercups elsewhere.

MALLOW,
COUNTY CORK

In the eighteenth century, when Mallow was a fashionable spa, there was a certain amount of hooliganism in the town. A contemporary song described the behaviour of local ruffians:

Bowing, belling, dancing, drinking,
Breaking windows, cursing, sinking,
Always talking, never thinking –
Live the Rakes of Mallow.

The 'Rakes', according to Elizabeth Bowen, were noisy squireen playboys, or cadets of the greater families, 'unthinkably dreary'. Today, Mallow is more respectable, a centre for farming, marketing and sugar manufacture.

THE RIVER LEE, COUNTY CORK

At the Custom House, the River Lee divides, and the North Channel pushes off to the right. The ship tied up at Lower Quay on the South Channel has most probably come from abroad; last time I visited Cork there were ships there from Russia and Turkey. The water of the quays and wharves is up to 30 feet deep, with the result that big vessels can come into the heart of the city.

CORK CITY CENTRE
Cork or *Corkaigh* meaning
'marsh', was built on slob
created by the confluence of
the rivers Bride and Lee,
meeting at high tide. Over
the years the marshes were
united and the channels
between them covered to
form the main streets. Today
the city centre is 'strewn like
a bouquet along the Lee
valley', according to Frank
O'Connor. Since I am not a
native of Cork – a desperate
status, as any Corkonian will
tell you – I cannot safely
identify the sweeping street
that dominates the picture.

BRIDGE OVER THE RIVER LEE, CORK CITY

Cork is a city of bridges over the divided river, a situation that encourages massive traffic jams. The ring road to west Cork, and the Dunkettle tunnel under the Lee, are supposed to make life easier. I am not sure if this bridge is near Coal Quay or not. In 1870, an anonymous Corkman, parodying the better-known Father Prout in the *Cork Examiner*, compared Coal Quay favourably with Versailles. He went on:

> *When at that ferry whence*
> *black Charon's wherry,*
> *Shall bear me, marry o'er*
> *the river Styx.*
> *Could I when parting choose*
> *the point of starting,*
> *My lovely Coal Quay is the*
> *place I'd fix.*

ST FINN BARRE'S CATHEDRAL, CORK CITY

St Finn Barre's three French-Gothic spires leap towards the heavens. The Protestant cathedral, designed by William Burges, was built during the 1860s. The Church of Ireland ran out of money, so that its length, at 163 feet, is a good deal shorter than that of the main central spire, at 240 feet. The anomaly does not make the richly ornamented building less beautiful. The Gothic dream of St Finn Barre's has been described as one of the wonders of Ireland – rightly in my opinion.

CORK ESTUARY

Like Dublin, Waterford and
Limerick, Cork is a Norse
foundation at the lowest ford
of a river. Here the River Lee
approaches Blackrock on its
right bank, before making a
turn into Lough Mahon, after
which it will enter the
expanse of Cork Harbour.

FUNFAIR AT KINSALE, COUNTY CORK

Circuses like Duffys and Fossetts still visit the small towns of Ireland during the summer months. Nowadays, the acts they offer are of the highest quality, since many performers come from Russia and Eastern Europe, where the circus culture has gone into decline since the ending of the Cold War. This looks more like a funfair – either way, it is amusement for the children.

KINSALE, COUNTY CORK

Kinsale (*Cionn tSailse* in Irish, meaning the 'Head of the Sea') is a seaport at the mouth of the Bandon River west of Cork, with many fine eighteenth-century houses built by captains and merchant princes. Thirty years ago the old town was in decay; among the ruinous houses you would see old women walking in handsome Kinsale cloaks. Today, much of the town's prosperity is brought by tourists and yachtsmen – you might call the place 'Kinsail'.

There is a little museum, which contains relics from the *Lusitania,* which was torpedoed off the Old Head in 1915. Bodies were washed up all along the coast; an old man told me: 'I remember the grand brown shoes they had on them after being sunk – to us at that time shoes were the greatest luxury.'

COASTLINE NEAR BALLYDEHOB, COUNTY CORK

I can guess where this little harbour is – somewhere between Ballydehob and Schull. On a fine day, when the sea is this shining blue, who needs the Mediterranean? That is what we say every time we holiday here – until we try to swim in the icy water.

BALTIMORE, COUNTY CORK

From Baltimore the sea stretches westward towards Roaringwater Bay where there are supposed to be a hundred islands, known as Carbury's Isles. It is difficult to determine how the hundred figure is reached without counting a good many little rocks. Most of the islands are flat. Only three are now inhabited: Cape Clear, Sherkin and Hare Island. The hill in the distance is Mount Gabriel, copper was mined on its slopes in Neolithic times, and the remains of the mines are still to be seen.

SLIEVE MISKISH MOUNTAINS AND BEAR ISLAND, COUNTY CORK

The Slieve Miskish, together with the Caha range, cover the northern side of Bantry Bay. There are still small farms there; I met an old man who, during the economic war in the 1930s, used to drive his cattle over hill paths to Bantry Fair, and then back again when they were unsold.

Off Bear Island, the British fleet used to anchor battleships like *The Lion, Agamemnon, Hercules* and *Superb*; the noise they made with their guns used to make the Delft rattle on the dresser. Until 1939 Castletown Bearhaven was a Treaty Port, and the British continued to maintain a garrison on Bear Island, posting a destroyer in Bantry Bay.

Castletown Bearhaven has a natural harbour with Bear Island protecting it from the southwestern winds and the currents that sweep in from the mouth of Bantry Bay. The town developed in the nineteenth century, beside some of the richest fishing grounds in the Atlantic. But fish are capricious: first the pilchards were there to be caught, but then they

vanished; later the herring and sprat appeared, and next they, too, disappeared without reason. Their place was taken by mackerel, which was caught in massive numbers, pickled, and sent to America in barrels. Now the south-western fishing fleet, together with the fishing boats of Europe, forlornly cast their nets for what is left.

**Signal Tower,
Toe Head,
County Cork**

This signal tower on Toe
Head is one of a series built
after the French invasion of
Bantry Bay at high places
around the coast up to
Donegal. They are linked
visually, the idea being that
warning beacons would be
lit, from one peak to another,
if the French ever came
again. They never did, but
these dour towers in windy
places remain, most of them
in ruins.

WHIDDY ISLAND OIL TERMINAL, BANTRY BAY, COUNTY CORK

I was present in 1971, when Jack Lynch, the Taoiseach, and the senior officials of Gulf Oil opened the terminal in pouring rain. For several years afterwards, unwieldy oil tankers, the biggest vessels in the world, turned into Bantry Bay, occasionally spilling some of their cargo. Then, in January 1979 came tragedy, when the French oil tanker, the *Betelgeuse,* exploded, and over 50 people died. The bay was an arena, and from all sides people viewed the flames. Now the storage tanks are used as fish farms, as you can see in this photograph.

BETWEEN TOE HEAD AND BALTIMORE, COUNTY CORK

Not far from Toe Head is Bean Cliff, whose name is derived from the same Gaelic word that named Beany Cliff in Cornwall, where Thomas Hardy courted his Emma. 'The opal and the sapphire of that wandering western sea' are here too.

**Two Boats in
Difficulties,
Castletown
Bearhaven,
County Cork**

Lucretius wrote and Dryden
translated:

> *Tis pleasant, safely to behold*
> *from shore*
> *The rolling ship and hear the*
> *tempest roar.*

Jason Hawkes may have felt
like that when viewing these
vessels in difficulties.

**KILLARNEY,
COUNTY KERRY**

The town in the foreground
is dwarfed by the splendours
of Macgillicuddy's Reeks
rising beyond Lough Leane,
the 'Lower Lake', which
covers 5,000 acres of water.

KILLARNEY,
COUNTY KERRY

Killarney has been a place for
tourists since the eighteenth
century, when Lord Kenmare
rebuilt the town and
encouraged visitors to this
remote place in Kerry to
view the lakes and mountains.
For some it was too far: Mrs
Delany wrote, 'I am very
desirous to see this enchanted
place, but it lies permanently
out of my way'.

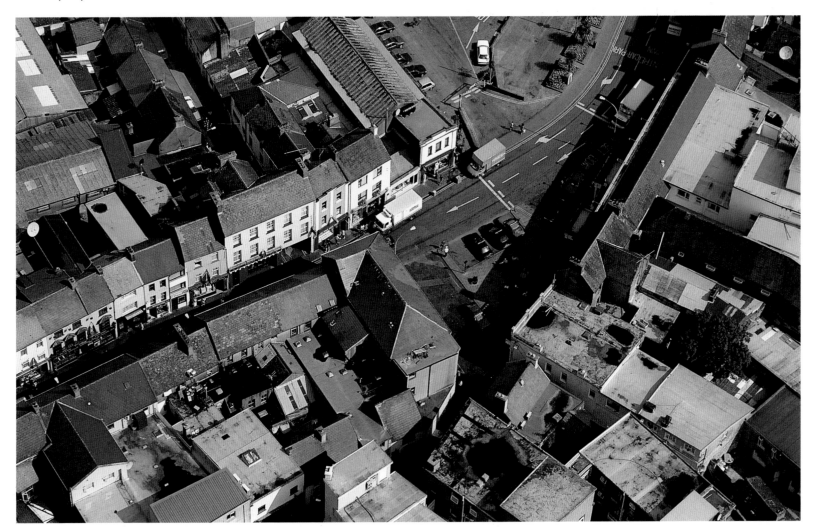

ROSS CASTLE, LOUGH LEANE AND MACGILLICUDDY'S REEKS, COUNTY KERRY

Beyond Lough Leane and Macgillicuddy's Reeks, there is a glimpse of Muckross Lake; beyond is the Upper Lake, where according to Dorothea Herbert, who was rowed there in 1786, 'the Rocks and Mountains are piled in such grand confusion that they set the head quite giddy to look at them'. Half a century later, Alfred, Lord Tennyson visited Killarney and, having seen Ross Castle situated on an island in Lough Leane, wrote 'The Splendour Falls on Castle Walls'.

KENMARE RIVER, COUNTY KERRY

I lived for some years on an island in the Kenmare River. During 50 years this fiord has not changed much: there are still dolphins and porpoises to be seen, as well as the odd sunfish; I remember a school of killer whales charging up towards Kenmare. At the sea end there are three rocks, known as the Bull, the Cow and the Calf.

These views of pewter-coloured sea, sun and cloud near the Kenmare River confirm my belief that here is one of the most beautiful places in the world.

KENMARE RIVER, LOOKING INLAND, COUNTY KERRY

The Kenmare 'river' is not a river at all, but a drowned valley 30 miles in length reaching upward to the town of Kenmare, which is situated at its head. It runs between a series of magnificent mountain ranges separating the Iveragh Peninsula from the Caha Peninsula, which overlooks another great fiord, Bantry Bay.

COWS IN A FIELD NEAR KILLARNEY, COUNTY KERRY

These cows, scattered like grains of sand, appear to be Friesians. Sixty years ago a rich meadow like this would have been grazing shorthorns, which was the favoured breed throughout Ireland, both for dairying and meat. The wild mountain farms in the uplands would have kept black Kerry cows, which were not much larger than ponies, and which flourished on poor soil and gave good, rich milk. Kerry cows are survivors of pre-medieval Irish cattle types, and existed in Neolithic times.

ADARE MANOR AND GARDENS, COUNTY LIMERICK

Adare Manor was rebuilt in the mid-nineteenth century by the 2nd Earl of Dunraven. The Earl was bored, being prevented by gout from hunting and fishing; he was also rich, since his wife was an heiress. He designed most of the Tudor fantasy by himself, although a few other architects, including Pugin, contributed. The photograph shows the house, with its Irish, battlemented spire, standing beside the River Maigue. To the left (outside the picture) at the gates of the manor, is Adare, a pretty village built by the Dunravens for their tenants.

Adare Manor was sold in 1985, and is now a hotel. The new proprietors have kept the box garden trim, and it looks well on this summer's day. On the south side of the manor is an inscription in giant letters on a stone tablet which says: 'This goodly house was erected by Windham Henry, Earl of Dunraven and Caroline his Countess without borrowing, selling or leaving a debt AD 1850.' There is also an inscription saying: 'Except the Lord build the house, their labour is but lost that build it.' Such vaingloriousness is not visible from the air.

THE SHANNON, COUNTY LIMERICK

A careless tailor has been cutting Ireland in two. The nineteenth-century traveller, John Forbes, considered the Shannon sublime: 'No one could contemplate this grand mass of water sweeping calmly and silently onwards without feeling that he is looking at something more than beauty.'

RIVER SHANNON, COUNTY LIMERICK

Here the Shannon travels through a landscape which Anthony Trollope described as 'soft and spewy'. The lordly river rises in the Culclough Mountains at a pool called Shannon Pot, which is as brown as Ireland's favourite drink. Along its journey to the sea, it passes through a series of lakes, strung like beads on a necklace: Lough Allen, Lough Ree and Lough Derg. Below Limerick, it sweeps down to its great mouth, between Kerry Head and Loop Head.

THURLES, COUNTY TIPPERARY

Thurles, built on the River Suir, is the cathedral town of the archdiocese of Cashel and Emly. The Cathedral of the Assumption, visible at the bottom right, was built in the 1860s by the prolific ecclesiastical architect known as J. J. McCarthy, the 'Irish Pugin'. The façade was modelled on that of Pisa Cathedral. The town is in sugar beet country, and during the winter the beet is piled high on the roads round about like piles of skulls. Archbishop Croke founded the Gaelic Athletic Association here in 1884. He is buried in the cathedral and there is a statue of him in the town.

TIPPERARY TOWN

Tipperary is situated on the River Ara in the Golden Vale, south of the Galtee mountains. The name of the town, and the county, immortalized in song, derives from *Tiobraid Arann* (the Well of Ara). Although Tipperary was founded by King John, who had a castle built here, the layout of the town, including the church, is nineteenth century.

TEMPLEMORE, COUNTY TIPPERARY
Here the fomer British Military Barracks has been adapted as the training centre for the *Garda Siochana* – Ireland's police force. Traces of the 'big church', *an Teampall Mór*, which gave the town its name, can be seen in the town's park. The writer George Borrow lived here for a time, and described the surrounding countryside in *Lavengro*. Behind the town is the Devil's Bit mountain with a great piece near the summit bitten out by the devil or eroded by glaciation, whichever you care to believe.

GALTEE MOUNTAINS, COUNTY TIPPERARY
Beyond the rich, green pastures of Tipperary rise the Galtees. You can follow a ridge walk along the top of the range, past some little lakes, and there is little of Munster you won't see. A less strenuous way of enjoying the Galtees is to drive from Dublin to Cork; between Cahir and Mitchelstown they loom above the main road.

LOUGHMOE CASTLE, TEMPLEMORE, COUNTY TIPPERARY

Loughmoe Castle is a fifteenth-century castle which, in the seventeenth century, was enlarged into a castellated mansion by the Purcell family, who were Gaelicized Anglo-Normans; this picture illustrates the change like an architectural drawing. With its mullioned and transomed windows, Loughmoe is what every true ruin should be: romantic, beautiful, difficult to find, and hard to reach, over boggy fields, with some barbed wire to deter you further.

TIPPERARY TOWN

Tipperary's most prominent native son was the Fenian, John O'Leary, who, after a weary nine years in English prisons, became a hero of Irish nationalists and writers, including Yeats. The poet included 'O'Leary's noble head' in his list of 'beautiful lofty things'.

COLLECTING SEAWEED, COUNTY WATERFORD

The people in wellies gathering seaweed in Dungarvan harbour could be working in a rice paddy; this is probably a species of sea lettuce. Recently, the Japanese have taken to importing Irish seaweed. Edible seaweeds include carrageen (*chondrus cruspus*) slioke or laver (*porphyra*), dulse (*rhodymenia*) and dulaman, which, during famine times, was used as a substitute for potatoes.

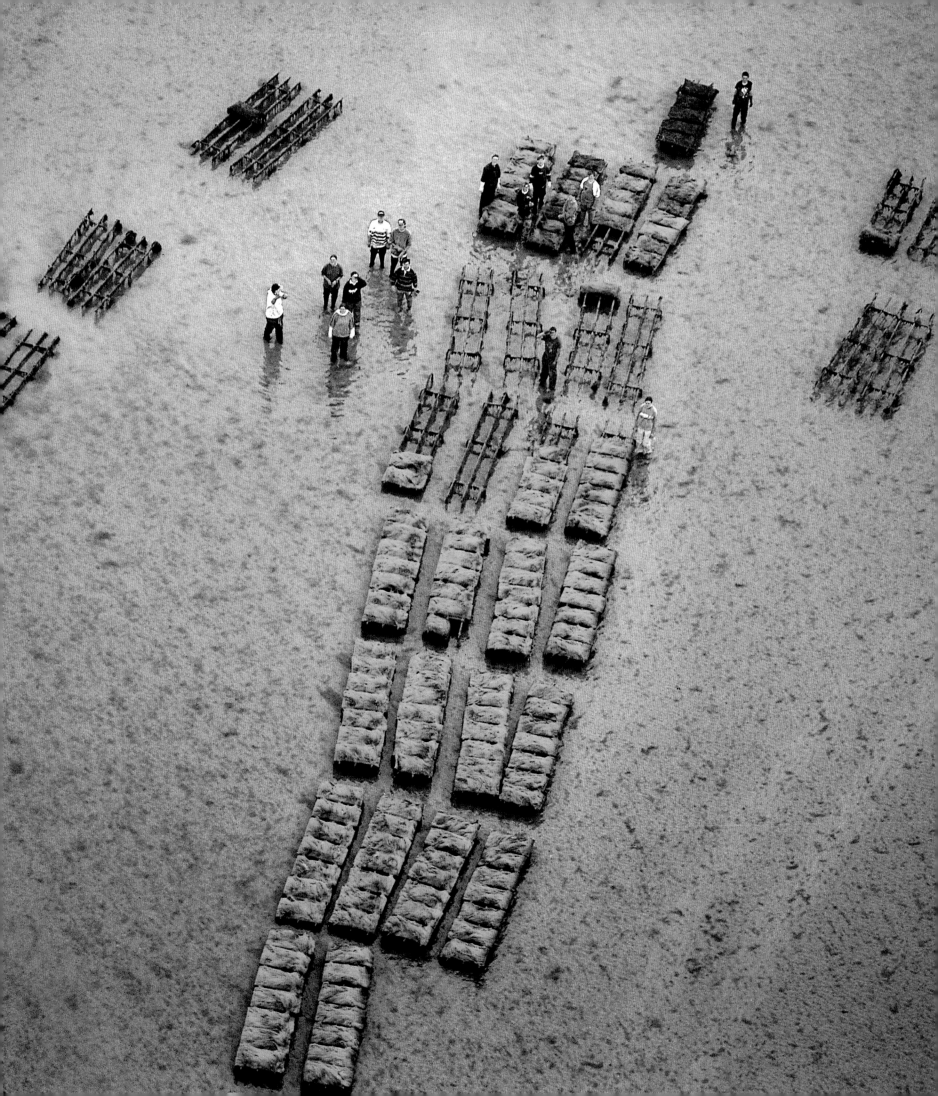

CONNACHT

....

'*COMME IL EST SAUVAGE*', SAID THE
FRENCH TOURIST WITH
SATISFACTION. HE HAD FOUND
MOUNTAINS AND BOGS, WINDSWEPT
COASTS, INNUMERABLE LAKES AND
RIVERS, AND HAD VISITED THE
ARAN ISLANDS ON A DAY WHEN
THEY WERE NOT OVERRUN WITH
TOURISTS. WHEN THE STRANGER
THINKS OF IRELAND, HE IS OFTEN
THINKING OF THE TERRITORY WEST
OF THE SHANNON, WHICH IS
ASSOCIATED WITH THE SCENT OF
TURF OR THE SMOKY LINE OF
THE TWELVE PINS.

The tourists' image of the five counties that make up Connacht as being the most 'Irish' part of Ireland is hard to shake off. He has heard of Yeats' country, Joyce country, Galway of the 12 tribes, Lady Gregory's Coole, Moore Hall and Connemara. Hell and Connacht are no longer equated.

For centuries the beauty of the west of Ireland was associated with extreme poverty; it was a natural place of exile. Early poetry was filled with mention of the wind in the glens, and wolf packs howling in the mountains as they chased the seven-horned deer. The beautiful land was, however, unproductive: the struggle for survival on the stones of Aran or the boggy fields of Leitrim and Roscommon was never easy, and the western Connacht suffered the evils of destitution and emigration more than any other province. Poverty is still a threat, although the returning emigrant who flies regularly into Knock and departs a week or two later for Birmingham or London may be impressed by signs of new prosperity. Equally, he knows that in the scattered, rurally based communities where small farms predominate, opportunities are strictly limited.

But the region has been transformed immeasurably since the time in the 1920s when Harold Speakman described Connemara as 'a land of red petticoats and a thousand wrinkled faces'. The grandeur of Robert Flaherty's Aran, and the whimsy of 'The Quiet Man' have been exchanged for a hard-headed realism. Tourism has become sophisticated. In the beautiful places, towns and villages have changed, together with people's lives. Holiday homes threaten to destroy the poetry of the heather and rocks and diminish the effects of the cauliflower-like clouds which Paul Henry used to paint. Thatched cottages are hard to find, as are curraghs and hookers. There are no more red petticoats on Inishmaan, and the Aran sweater is now hung on a coat hanger for the tourist to buy.

'The trouble with Galway is that it stands in a closer relationship with a Gaelic hinterland than any other Irish city', Frank O'Connor wrote 30 years ago. In those days the wild hinterland of Connemara was on the city's doorstep, and it seemed that the days had not long gone since the prayer 'From the ferocious O'Flahertys good Lord deliver us' had fervent meaning. But although the city has swollen, and the suburbs around Galway Bay appear to be endless, Galway remains the gateway to Connemara. The road west leads by Lough Corrib towards the area where the Twelve Pins and the Maam mountains joust for space. At one time, the terrain made the journey almost impossible; in the eighteenth century one gentleman used to bring two footmen carrying a net to put over the bog to allow him to walk over.

In the nineteenth century, Maria Edgeworth had to be

carried across the 'slough' by a giant named Ulike Burke in order to reach Ballinahinch Castle and its 40-mile-long avenue. The castle, now a hotel, is still there, in the heart of Connemara, whose name derived from the *Conmaicne* or 'Tribe of the Sea'. Clifden is regarded as Connemara's capital, but it is Maam Cross that is called 'the centre of everything and everything comes in due course to Maam Cross', according to Somerville and Ross. It points the way to Lough Corrib and Lough Mask; to the coast and the harbour for the Aran Islands. And from Maam, too, you can go to Mayo. Mayo remains lonely and wild: Sitka plantations fur the hills, and the turf has been stripped by machinery along the west coast from Achill to Belmullet, but the mountains of Nephin Beg, Mweelrea, and Partry are unscarred and unchanged. Jason Hawkes has recorded in particular the beauty of Lough Mask and Lough Carra.

North of Achill, above Killala on the lonely coastline stretching from Benwee Head to Downpatrick, traces of Neolithic man have been found and exploited at the Ceide Fields, where a show of early field systems is on display. Anyone visiting this heritage centre will question why early man should have chosen to carve out these small fields and settle in a place exposed to the changing cycles of Mayo's weather. Less exposed, but still a moving tribute to the fortitude of men and women, is the deserted village of Slievemore on Achill Island, once a 'booley', or place for cattle pasture, a village that was only abandoned in the nineteenth century.

Beside Westport rises the 2,510-foot-high white cone of Croagh Patrick. On Garland Sunday, the last Sunday in July, pilgrimages – sometimes as many as 40,000 people – climb to its summit. Whether the origins of this holy climb should be considered pagan or as deriving from the missionary activities of St Patrick is in doubt. However, in Sligo, no one climbing Knocknarea, which is topped by a stone cairn, known as 'Maeve's Lump', can be in doubt that here we are in contact with older gods.

Sligo has more pre-Christian monuments and sites than any place in Ireland. Near Knocknarea is the Neolithic cemetery of Carrowmore; there is also Heapstown, the Neolithic tombs at Keshcorran, and hundreds of lonely, wedge-shaped tombs and portal dolmens elsewhere. Yeats was conscious of the area's pagan presence, while Frank O'Connor called Sligo 'a poet's country'. There is really only one poet of Sligo; Yeats has made all too familiar the beautiful names of Sligo, Innisfree, Lough Gill, Drumcliffe, Glencar and Lissadell.

Leitrim could do with a well-known poet. The county, which is thin as a sausage, 46 miles long, with a maximum breadth of 18 miles, has tended to be ignored by travellers, as having 'no particular feature or comment'. But although it lacks the drama of other counties in Connacht, Leitrim has a little bit of everything: pleasant farming country, plenty of lakes, small, tussocky hills, where the living is hard, and even a little bit of coastline reaching into Donegal Bay, as though the county had to have a toe in the sea. Here you can seek out some of the hidden wonders of Ireland: the Black Pig Dyke between Lough Melvin and Upper Lough Macnean in Fermanagh; O'Rourke's Table, a flat-topped hill near Dromahair Fenagh; and the Corracloona Grave, hidden in the heather.

Many years ago I sought out Leitrim – the town. I had travelled in winter in the path of Donal Cam O'Sullivan Beare, the sixteenth-century warrior, whose flight with a thousand companions from County Cork to Leitrim is an epic of Irish history. I walked the route in winter, seeking out the final place where Donal Cam had found refuge. The name meant much to me, and I had built up Leitrim into something substantial. On that January day I eventually found a dozen or so houses, a few shops and pubs, and a monument to the man who had marched across Ireland pursued by his foes. 'Leitrim? You could spend a pound in it', the barman said, drawing a much-needed pint as I took off another layer of damp clothing and presented him with my broken umbrella. Leitrim was all round me, and it felt wonderful.

Leitrim shares the Shannon with Roscommon, and they both benefit from what is probably the least disruptive aspect of modern tourism – boating. The Shannon swells with lakes and waterways, and the boats charge up and down them. During the summer months, towns like Boyle and Carrick-on-Shannon are thriving boating centres, and the Shannon has become a summer lifeline in an area of struggling small farms and failing businesses.

To the east of Connacht, the scenery of Roscommon has a still and gentle charm compared to the wildness of Mayo and Galway. This sense of not advertising its treasures makes them all the more rewarding for having to discover them. Lough Key, and its forest park, which offers wide views over the lake, Boyle Abbey and the recently restored Strokestown Park House, as well as the lonely tower house of Glinsk, are all worth seeking out.

On the plain of Roscommon is a remote area associated with pagan gods and Maeve, goddess and queen, in particular. At Knocknarea she flaunts herself. Here at Rathcroghan, however, a few miles from the road between Frenchpark and Tulsk on the way to Westport, her presence has to be sought among the most remarkable, yet almost unknown, pagan locations in these islands. Cruachan was the royal seat of the kings of Connacht, where they were crowned. Maeve had a place here, and Conn of the Hundred Battles. Eire, Fodhla and Banba are supposed to lie in the Reillig na Riogh – the graveyard of kings. For good measure, there is a little cave nearby called Owneygrat, the 'Cave of the Cats', which is an entrance to the underworld.

Jason Hawkes did not fly over Owneygrat, which, together with the kings' grounds at Cruachan, would not be camera-friendly from the air – appearing only as a little series of humps and bumps. But his camera has caught the essence of Connacht in a series of patterned seascapes and waterscapes, and has captured much of the drama of the province, which the earthbound traveller would have trouble seeking out.

GALWAY CITY

Since Galway city provides a good base from where to set out for Connemara and Mayo, it attracts a huge number of tourists during the summer months. They find a particular atmosphere and character in a city that boasts its own unique cultural identity.

DISUSED RAILWAY AND ROAD BRIDGE, COUNTY MAYO

The road between Ballinrobe and Claremorris resembles a snake which has engulfed the railway beneath it. A long time has passed since trains ran this way. I do not know precisely when the road took over the function of this particular branch of the Midland Great Western line, which was amalgamated with Coras Iompar Eirann when the railways were nationalized in 1946. Claremorris, however, still has a main line linking it with Dublin and Westport.

LOUGH MASK,
COUNTY MAYO

Lough Mask is a grey lake full of fish, ten miles long by four wide, with two arms. Its eastern shore a maze of pitted limestone and turloughs (lakes on limestone that flood or disappear altogether according to season). In the nineteenth century a canal was built to link it with Lough Corrib – another huge fisherman's paradise. Unfortunately the engineers failed to remember that limestone is porous and the water flowing into it sank through the rock.

ISLAND IN LOUGH CARRA, COUNTY MAYO

From this island, the chimneys of ruined Moore Hall, surrounded by forestry, are visible. The house was burnt down in 1922. The arsonists saved some church vestments that had come from Spain, but everything else was destroyed. In the nineteenth century, the water for the house was brought from the lake in a cart drawn by a mule all day long. When the maids had filled their cans, the cart went down to the lake again. Later George Moore installed a pump, which cost him £200.

LOUGH CARRA, COUNTY MAYO

Lough Carra is an irregularly shaped lake about six miles long, and never more than one mile wide. George Moore described it in his novel, *The Lake*. Although Lough Mask and Lough Carra are situated beside each other, and linked by a little river, the Keel, they are quite different. Lough Mask is a grim and grey sheet of water, while the chalk bottom of Lough Carra gives it a luminous green colour.

**STORM OVER
LOUGH MASK,
COUNTY MAYO**

The storm brings to mind the
troubles of Captain Boycott,
Lord Erne's agent, whose
little house stands beside
Lough Mask Castle on the
eastern shore of the lake. In
1880, after the Captain was
sent to Coventry, and no one
would harvest his crops, a
workforce of 50 Orangemen
came down from Cavan to
undertake the task. They
were escorted by a thousand
troops. The enterprise cost
the government an estimated
£10,000, or, in Parnell's
words, 'one shilling for every
turnip dug from Boycott's
land'. It was the *Daily Mail*
which first used the word
'boycott' as a verb.

**RYANAIR JET AT
KNOCK INTERNATIONAL
AIRPORT,
COUNTY MAYO**

Knock Airport is ten years
old, and its popularity has
confounded those sceptics
who believed that it would
prove a costly failure. Instead,
it has a busy role, linking the
west of Ireland to Europe and
America. For passengers and
pilgrims alike, its very
existence has a touch of the
miraculous that is additional to
the sacred images that
appeared on a church gable
not far away. Because this
airport is the result of one
man's obsession, the dream
of Monsignor Horan, its
planning is an exception to
any conventional airport.

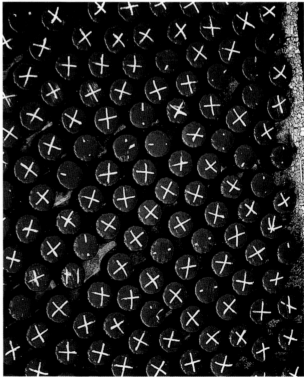

**HAY BALES,
COUNTY MAYO**
These hay bales, secured in
their black plastic covers,
look like a detachment
of Crusaders.

STONE WALLING,
COUNTY ROSCOMMON

Granite, limestone, erratics, old red sandstone, quartzite peaks, Silurian slates, basalts, and millstone grits are all ingredients in Ireland's stony mix. 'Stones in every fertile place', John Betjeman observed when cycling in Ireland in the 1940s. Since then, the bulldozer has come in to make the big fields. But although stones may be pushed into a corner, they endure. Before the bulldozer, the best way to make a space among the stones was to build walls; a labour that became an art form. Dry-stone walling differs little from the walls built in Neolithic times.

BOYLE,
COUNTY ROSCOMMON

The River Boyle which runs by the town, is linked to two lakes – Lough Gara and Lough Key. The camera is looking over the town, northeastward, to the diamond-shaped Lough Key. One of the islands is Castle Island – a seat of the MacDermotts – where the *Annals of Lough Cé* were compiled. King House, the eighteenth-century seat of the King family, is visible; unusually, for a big house in Ireland, it was built in the centre of a town. After the Kings deserted it for a more salubrious location at Rockingham, on the shores of Lough Key, King House became a barracks, then a semi-ruin. Recently it has been restored.

BOYLE ABBEY, COUNTY ROSCOMMON

Boyle Abbey is a Cistercian foundation, a daughter house of Mellifont. No part of the building dates from later than the thirteenth century, but since it took 60 years to build, its architecture is varied, being both Romanesque and Gothic. The pillars, of coursed ashlar, have wonderful carvings on the capitals, of men, beasts and foliage, but we are too high up to see them.

Cromwellian soldiers stabled their horses here, as was their custom, and carved their names on the doors. In the eighteenth century, the ruin was covered in ivy, and belonged to the Misses Robertson, in whose garden it was situated. Now the ivy has been stripped away, and the abbey is in the hands of the Board of Public Works.

INISHEER,
ARAN ISLANDS,
COUNTY GALWAY

Inisheer, the most southerly of
the Aran Islands, can be reached
from Doolin on the Clare coast.
Since it is not as suffused with
tourism as Inishmore, you can
get some feeling here of what
life used to be like in these
harsh and beautiful islands.
The playwright, John Synge
was rowed to Inisheer in a
three-oared '*curragh*' in high
seas: 'The black curragh
working slowly through this
world of grey, and the soft
hissing of the rain gave me one
of the moods in which we
realise with immense distress the
short moment we have left us
to experience all the wonder
and beauty of the world.'

GALWAY CITY

In the bottom left-hand corner is part of University College, Galway. The road leads to the vast cathedral of Our Lady Assumed into Heaven and St Nicholas, built through the determination of Bishop Browne between 1957 and 1965. The site was that of the old city gaol, where many patriots were imprisoned. Beyond is a glimpse of the Galway River and, in the distance Galway Bay. Nowadays there are too many suburbs around the city for you, in the words of Bing Crosby, to enjoy hanging around watching the sun go down.

GALWAY CITY

The river is the Galway River that has a short life, flowing into Galway Bay. At the Salmon Weir Bridge you can watch the salmon pass upwards towards Lough Corrib. Today there is a new prosperity in the city of the 'Tribes', an expanding university, and an increasing industrial base.

GALWAY CITY

Galway has managed to retain, almost intact, a maze of narrow, winding streets that reflect its gentlemanly, mercantile past. You can walk around this centre in a morning. In medieval times, Galway was an important trading port with a flourishing wine trade conducted between France and Spain. The rulers of this city-state were families of Anglo-Norman descent including the 12 'Tribes': Blake, Lynch, Browne, Bodkin Kirwan, French, Martins, and so on. They oversaw Galway's wealth and expansion until the disaster of the Cromwellian wars.

CARRICK-ON-
SHANNON,
COUNTY LEITRIM

From the marina at Carrick-
on-Shannon, you can go by
water every which way: up
the Boyle River to Lough
Key, or along the Shannon,
upstream to Lough Allen, or
downstream towards
Lough Ree.

RIVER SHANNON,
COUNTY LEITRIM

There is only one cruiser on
this beautiful stretch of the
Shannon. In mid season you
would expect to find half a
dozen or more racing up and
down. You can hire a boat,
an expensive business, step in,
and without any sort of
qualification turn the key and
head off through lake and
river and all the complexities
of the Shannon waterway.
Hopefully the weather will be
fine. In rain you pull in at the
nearest town and nearest pub.

CARRICK-ON-SHANNON,
COUNTY LEITRIM

Once the town had a reputation for being fiercely Protestant. It is good that boating has taken over from bigotry; the unpolluted river, the largest in the British Isles, with its string of navigable lakes, is ideal for sailing.

SLIGO TOWN
(FAR RIGHT)

With its wide harbour and Victorian streets and houses, Sligo has a proud history. Its origins are associated with the fiercest of Norman barons, William de Burgo and Maurice Fitzgerald. There are two cathedrals, a fine Dominican priory, and the courthouse, town hall, library and museum are worth visiting. But the town hall has come to accept the fact that its chief fame arises because Yeats' brothers spent their holidays there. While they stayed with their grandfather, William Pollexfen, in a house 'so big that there was always room to hide in', the poet learned about fairies and ghosts, and the painter absorbed views of the ships and quaysides.

ESTUARY, SLIGO TOWN

The sea gave Sligo its prosperity, by way of both trade and fishing. The poet, W. B. Yeats' relations, the Pollexfens, were seafaring merchants and ship owners. Fishing was declining even in Yeats' day: his 'Old Fisherman' meditated how,

The herring are not in the tides as they were of old;
My sorrow! for many a creak gave the creel in the cart,
That carried the take to Sligo town to be sold,
When I was a boy with never a crack in my heart.

SLIGO TOWN

The River Garavogue has
flowed down from Lough
Gill through the town and
has entered Sligo Bay. It is
a watery place. Frank
O'Connor quotes a friend
leaning over the old bridge
crossing the Garavogue and
quoting: 'I would that we
were, my beloved, white
swans on the foam of the
sea! There's enough water
here to wash all the water
closets in Sligo!'

BEN BULBEN,
COUNTY SLIGO

Sligo Bay is enclosed by the Knocknarea and Ben Bulben mountains like a book between bookends. This is Ben Bulben, a cliffed block of carboniferous limestone, 525 metres high. Its top is not bare, as Yeats wrote, but covered in blanket bog. Ben Bulben is a nunatek – an island peak – which, during the ice age was high enough to rise above the ice. (The word *nunatek* is Eskimo, and comes from Greenland.) The plants that still cling to the cliffs' edges, like saxifrage and mountain avens, escaped the effects of the ice age; Jason Hawkes' camera is almost near enough to pick them out. A less rugged way of viewing such alpine-arctic plants would be to visit the Burren.

SLIEVE GAMPH, OR
OX MOUNTAINS,
COUNTY SLIGO
The Ox Mountains are
mostly in the south of Sligo,
although a little of the southwestern range crosses into
Mayo. They are hills rather
than mountains, monotonous
– even in outline – boggy,
and with a good deal of
forestry. The camera has
made them a distant backdrop
to the pattern of fields in the
foreground.

OWENMORE RIVER, COUNTY SLIGO

The Owenmore River rises in the Iron Mountains, and then flows to join the Shannon near Dowra. Here it is far bigger than the Shannon, which, at this stage, is just a trickle. Together they flow into the first of the Shannon lakes, Lough Allen, which can be glimpsed in the upper left of this picture.

WATER LILIES, COUNTY SLIGO

Water lilies fur the lake, making it look like a worn carpet. A current, a spring, or some hostile movement, has kept a circle of green water clear. Lilies grow in still water, pools, lakes and at the river's edge.

TOBERCURRY,
COUNTY SLIGO

The name Tobercurry derives from the Gaelic *Tobar an Choire*, the 'Well of the Cauldron'. Little farms surround it. Once the town had a railway station, once it had a fair; more recently, a shoe factory. And the Moylough Belt, an eighth-century saint's relic, was found nearby. In the distance beyond the River Moy, the line of the Ox Mountains is visible.

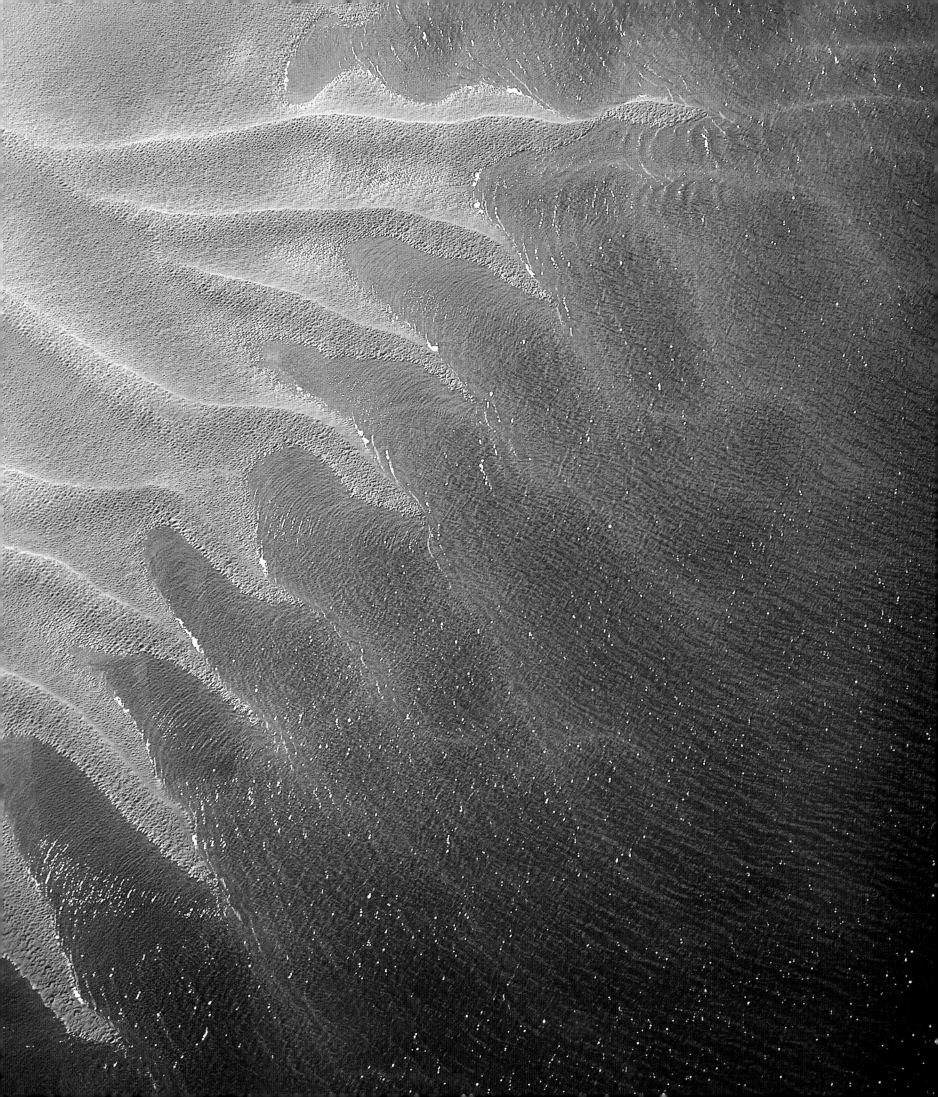

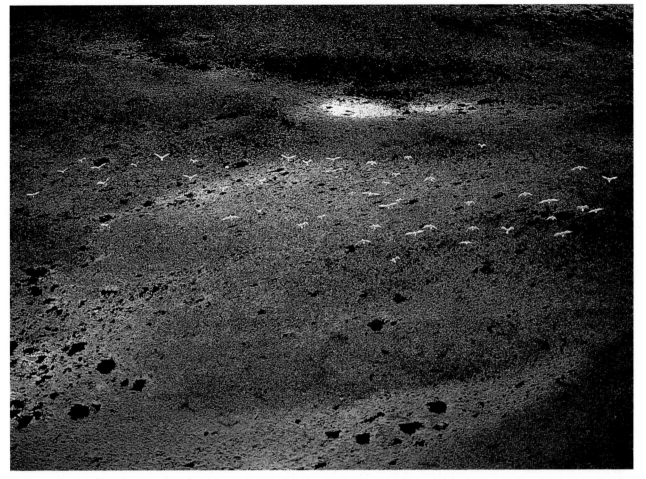

**SEAGULLS ON THE
STRAND,
COUNTY SLIGO**

You would have to go
northwards, up to Bundoran,
to see as many people as there
are birds on this Sligo strand.
In Bundoran you will find a
golf course, tennis courts,
chip shops and ice-cream
parlours, and all the gaiety
you need to help pass a
windswept, rainy day in July
and August. The seagulls
down in Sligo have made
their own crowd, but picked
a quieter, not easily accessible,
place with a salt marsh
behind it.

**BALLISODARE BAY,
COUNTY SLIGO**

Ballisodare Bay is situated at
the foot of Knocknarea. Here
are the waters and the wild.
This is Yeats' country:

> *Cuchulain stirred,*
> *Stared on the horses of*
> *the sea, and heard*
> *The cars of battle and his*
> *own name cried;*
> *And fought with the*
> *invulnerable tide.*

ULSTER

....

From northern outposts of Ulster, like Rathlin Island, or Fair Head, it seems that you only have to stretch out your fingers to touch Scotland. Across the Mull of Kintyre, Scottish farms gleam in the sun like sugar cubes; the divide is narrow, compared to the distance between Ireland and the Welsh coast, which faces Wicklow. The link to the greater island of the British Isles is a natural one.

The Vikings and Normans chose Leinster for the site of their invasions, but the first invaders crossed the narrower seas. Only 3,000 years after the last sheets of ice retreated and the ice age ceased, man made his first landing on Irish soil, following the same route (by sea) from Scotland that I took by air in a microlight. Eight thousand years ago, Larnian man left his flints and axes, and the bones and shells that were the remains of his meals, on the northwestern corner of Lough Neagh, and on the Antrim coast.

'As a result of its history, Ulster is unjustly neglected by the visitor – a fact which adds immeasurably to its attractions. '

Since then plenty of people from Scotland have left their imprint on the province; the stamp of the plantations and the work of the livery companies is still evident. The central 'diamond' which is a feature of so many Ulster towns including Donegal; the castles of Scottish Gothic style, and walled towns like Londonderry (or Derry, according to your political persuasion) and Coleraine give a different impression of Ireland's townscapes than those in the south. A traditional planter's town like Cookstown shows the planning that resulted in William Stewart's development, that took place in around 1650. A village like Eglington, on the shores of Lough Foyle, has a cricket pitch and a line of trees, each one planted to commemorate a coronation. You know you are not in any other of the three provinces.

Ulstermen tend to state that, in general, the north is better kept. The claim that the roads in the north are as smooth as satin, while those in the south are nothing but a series of potholes, is exaggerated. But there is a difference in landscape, which might just be equated with the virtues of hard work, independence and plain-speaking that are associated with Ulstermen, whether Catholic or Protestant. The values and worth of country life, which have a subtle influence on the look of the landscape, are reflected in the poetry of such countrymen as Seamus Heaney, John Hewitt and Patrick Kavanagh.

   . . . *So it's Ballinamallard, it's Crossmaglen*
   It's Augnacloy, it's Donahgadee,
   It's Magherafelt needs the best of men. . .
wrote John Hewitt.

   I take my stand by Ulster names,
   Each clean hard name like a weathered stone. . .

The Ulster farmer has favoured isolated farms and farmhouses, and the independence that comes with solitude. Each farm that might possess about 30 acres must have some sort of road access, so that much of the Ulster countryside is still a network of lanes, or 'loanings' skirting tiny fields.

There are other forces that affect the Ulster scenery in addition to a harsh climate and an unforgiving history. Industry made an impact in the north, which was not to be seen elsewhere on the island. The south has no nineteenth-century industrial towns like Belfast, where at one time 60,000 people were employed in the linen industry alone. Smoking chimney stacks, industrial complexes, as well as the shipyards, dominated a stretch of the eastern coastline. Physically, the heart of Ulster may be the area surrounding the Lough Neagh basin, but economically, even in the face of decline and unemployment, the hub of Ulster life has always been in the areas around Antrim and Down. As recently as 1961, 40 per cent of Ulster's working population were in industry, compared to 17 per cent in the south.

Industrial development was concentrated in east Ulster, which attracted the bulk of the province's population, while the west simultaneously lost its people. In the century and a half following the famine, the population of mid-Ulster and west Ulster, including the three counties in the Republic – Cavan, Monaghan and Donegal – went down by 60 per cent, while during the same period it went up by 30 per cent around Belfast. This drain of human resources has not ceased, as the decline of the fishing industry, the plight of the small hill-farmer and the lack of an industrial infrastructure continue to take their toll. There are brave exceptions, often in the face of violence, like the development of the area around Londonderry/Derry (perhaps it is easiest to refer to it as the Maiden City, but that sobriquet also has political overtones).

The developments of history, along with the harsh differences caused by tribal and religious conflict, have set Ulster apart from the rest of Ireland. Even the similarities breed differences: the Glens of Antrim, with their scattered farms and remote hills, have been compared to Wicklow, but something subtle in the atmosphere tells you that they are indubitably in the north; the same is true of the sheep-studded Mourne Mountains, with their deep valleys and forestry plantations. And yet the crazy, winding, straying border established nearly 80 years ago had made divisions that have little consequence in the natural world. The Upper and Lower Lough Erne, which stretch for miles, form an important artery between north and south. A bridge divides Stabane from Lifford in the Republic and thus also two ways of living and thinking, though in south Armagh a magician could not separate Ulster from the Republic in the tangle of hills and roads.

Political events have resulted in the unfamiliarity of many of Ulster's landscapes and landmarks to those outside the province. A bomb in London or Manchester may result in ten cancellations in a holiday hotel in Connemara, but a hundred at a similar establishment in the Six Counties. The tourist board's advertisements plead wistfully: 'You'll never know unless you go.' Indeed, otherwise there is much to miss in the diverse nature of the nine counties of Ulster – the contrast between the Dartry and Blue Stack mountains in Donegal and the rich lands of Armagh (known as the Orchard of Ulster), or the difference between a walk on One Man's Path on Slieve League and another along the flat shores of eel-filled Lough Neagh.

The Giant's Causeway may be famous enough in pictures, but for those who are affected by violent news, it remains, in Dr Johnson's words, 'worth seeing, but not worth going to see'. Other landmarks of Ulster remain almost unknown, like Slemish, the mountain where the young slave, Patrick, tended his flocks among the forests for six years; and Torr Head, near Cushendun, which looks across the sea to the Mull of Kintyre; as well as the granite pudding-like shape of Ailsa Craig. The waterways of the Upper and Lower Erne rival the Shannon, while Ulster boasts a lake as big as a county – Lough Neagh, the largest lake in the British Isles, at 150 miles in area. Its alternative name, Loch Neachnach, is perhaps onomatopoeic, taken from the neigh of horse-god Eochu, Lord of the Otherworld, which is believed to be situated beneath its waters.

Then, there are the man-made marvels of Ulster, like the eerie, double-headed, heart-shaped effigy, whose arms are like kangaroo's paws, that stands in the long grass of Caldvagh cemetery on Boa Island in County Fermanagh. The figure was probably carved in the seventh century, but seems to represent an older pagan world. The traveller cannot see the stone cashel of Grianan of Aileach near Derry, or Navan Fort or the Dorsey, the ramparts close by Navan Fort, since the fort itself has lost some of its romance after being converted into a heritage centre, without experiencing a feeling of wonder at the work of the ancient tribes. The landmarks of Ulster cross the centuries: Dunluce Castle on one cliff, for example, or the Temple of Mussenden on another. These should be sought out, together with the obscure Crom Castle, a plantation castle with ivy-covered towers on the shores of Lough Neagh. Or see the three-ramped, earthen fort of Dunglady on top of a hill near Maghera. Visit the curious result of a quarrel between Mr Bernard and Lady Anne Ward, which resulted in their mansion, Castleward, having two faces: the front classical, the back Gothic. Or see Waringstown's church, which was designed by an apprentice of Inigo Jones; or St Malachi's parish church at Hillsborough; or the dolmens – Legananny, Kilfeaghan, and Ossian's Grave.

As a result of its history, Ulster is unjustly neglected by the visitor – a fact which adds immeasurably to its attractions. Far more than the rest of visited and signposted Ireland, for the romantic traveller, Ulster is a place of wonder and discovery.

KILLYBEGS, COUNTY DONEGAL
From the harbour at Killybegs, you can look southward across Donegal Bay to the mountains of Mayo. The church of St Catherine dominates the little port. The saint is its patron, and, according to the Four Masters, she saved it from destruction in 1513. Niall Mor Mac Sweeney is buried here; on his tomb is a carving of a gallowglass – he was among the most ruthless of these mercenary soldiers.

ARMAGH CATHEDRAL

In Armagh there are two cathedrals, Catholic and Protestant, each claiming the name of Patrick, glaring at each other from rival hills, permanent symbols of discord.

This is the lofty, twin-towered Catholic cathedral built in the mid-nineteenth century from Armagh limestone and Dungannon freestone. It is yet another architectural exercise by J. J. McCarthy, 'the Irish Pugin', whose work was dominated by thoughts of Italy. Italian artists were called in to decorate the interior with flying angels.

NAVAN FORT, COUNTY ARMAGH

Navan Fort was the seat of ancient kings, the *Emain Macha* of Irish mythology. Here was the seat of Conchobar mac Nesa and his Red Branch Knights, the chief of whom was the doomed warrior Cuchulain. Beside the site of the 18-acre hillfort is a museum and theme park to evoke ancient Celtic legend.

ARMAGH CITY AND MARKET

Besides St Patrick's preference for Armagh, the city is significant because it lies at an important road junction on the Belfast–Enniskillen and Dundalk–Derry roads. Because of its strategic position, this tranquil-seeming town, with its pleasant Georgian architecture and tree-lined mall, has attracted plenty of strife over the centuries. It did not escape unscathed during the Troubles.

GWEEDORE, COUNTY DONEGAL

Gweedore stretches down from Bloody Foreland to the Gweebarra Bay estuary. A century and a half ago, a landlord named Lord George Hill bought 23,000 acres of this isolated area, which was almost totally outside English jurisdiction. Its Irish-speaking population clung to tradition, and lived in wretched poverty. In the years prior to the famine, Lord George abolished rundale (the traditional complex system of land division), built a harbour and established a shop that sold sealing wax, fish-hooks, scissors, Epsom salts and coffin nails. He also wrote a book describing his reforming experiments. Some people thought he was 'out to exterminate the Irish race'. Others approved, like Thomas Carlyle: 'In all Ireland I saw no such beautiful soul.' Carlyle noted the awful poverty of Gweedore just after the famine: 'Black huts . . . damp peat, black heather, grey stones and ragged desolation of men and things!' The poverty is thankfully gone, and the beauty of the area remains.

LANDSCAPE WITH DERRYVEAGH MOUNTAINS, COUNTY DONEGAL

Like the Blue Stacks, the stone that makes up the Derryveagh range, part of the mountain heartland of Donegal, is granite. Although the peaks are a good deal higher than the Blue Stacks, they share the soft, rounded look which contrasts with the quartzite cone of Errigal, right beside them. The highest mountain in the Derryveaghs is Slieve Snaght.

**GWEEBARRA BAY
ESTUARY,
COUNTY DONEGAL**
The Gweebarra River
meets the sea at low tide,
flowing into the estuary.
In the distance is
Gweebarra Bridge, linking
Lettermacaward with
southwestern Donegal and
the road to Glenties. There
is a two-mile-long, white
beach near here, called
Dooey. Lovely from the air,
lovely on the ground.

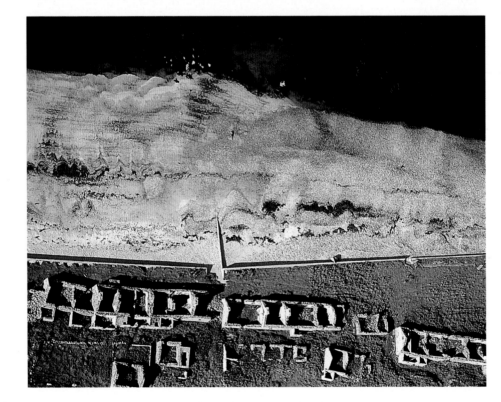

THE ROSSES, COUNTY DONEGAL

The Rosses in Donegal are not to be confused with Yeats' Rosses in Sligo. The Rosses of Donegal is a flat district in the far west of Donegal, between the Derryveagh mountains and the sea. *Na Rosa* in Gaelic, meaning 'The Headlands', is a sandy area, dotted with lakes and strewn with huge, bare rocks, known as 'erratics'. In parts of this stony land, it seems difficult to imagine that any sort of farming life could have been sustained, but the people of The Rosses were survivors. Their holdings averaged about two-and-a-half acres, of which one acre was devoted to potatoes, another to oats, and the rest to grazing. In summer, they took their cattle up the nearby mountains, while, part of their income came from 'American money'. But their real living derived from seasonal migration: every summer the able-bodied men went to Scotland, looking for employment. The unmarried girls and children also migrated to work in farms as far away as Tyrone and the Lagan Valley.

THE ROSSES,
COUNTY DONEGAL

In The Rosses the co-operative movement was pioneered by Patrick Gallagher, known as Paddy the Cope (or Co-op). As a boy of nine, he was employed by a Strabane farmer, who paid him £3 for six months' work. Single-handedly he founded the Templecrone Co-op Society in 1906, with a capital of £1.75. It is a reflection of the realism and self-sufficiency of the people of The Rosses that the Cope's Co-op flourished. The poverty of the area in the last century was highlighted by the visit in 1882 of the chief secretary, George Otto Trevelyan, who was in the process of implementing what was known as the 'Pinch of Hunger Policy'. This provided barely adequate relief measures in the face of failing harvests. Although he was struck by the misery of the cabins, the rags of the children, the meagre little potato patches between the rocks, and witnessed a newspaper stunt whereby he was shown a family who appeared to be dining on seaweed, Trevelyan refused to reopen any relief works. Luckily for the people of Donegal, the next harvest was a good one.

VALLEY ROAD FROM ARDARA TO GLENCOLUMBKILLE, COUNTY DONEGAL

This remote green valley is where St Columbkille (Columba) retired to wrestle with demons. On St Columbkille's Day, 9 July, a three-and-a-half-mile 'turas', or pilgrimage, takes place before sunrise, during which 15 stations near the village are visited, each of which is marked by early Christian and prehistoric remains. Like The Rosses, Glencolumbkille attracted the co-operative movement. Here its moving spirit was the remarkable Father McDyer, who died in 1987.

SLIEVE LEAGUE, COUNTY DONEGAL

Like Ben Bulben, Slieve League is a nunatek, hosting alpine-arctic flora. I have never found any here, being more concerned with keeping my head while navigating the fearsome One Man's Path, which is on a knife edge between a drop towards an inland lake among the Lair of Whirlwinds and another, on the seaward side, of over 1,500 feet.

The name of the highest point of Slieve League, the Eagle's Nest, is a reminder that this was the last haunt of the golden eagle in Ireland. The last sea eagle disappeared from Donegal around 80 years ago. In the early years of this century, Arthur Fox met an old woman who, as a baby, was said to have been carried off by a Slieve League eagle; her frantic mother managed to rescue her.

BLUE STACK MOUNTAINS, COUNTY DONEGAL

The Blue Stacks, which rise north of Donegal town upward from Lough Eske, are a range of granite hills. The granite, of a handsome pale-pink colour with a name of its own – Barnesmore – gives them a smooth appearance. They have none of the drama of quartzite formations elsewhere, like the snaggle-toothed Slieve League or the white cone of Errigal.

The Blue Stacks are strewn with sheep and pervaded with shepherds' lore. William Allingham filled his airy Donegal mountain with little men; their king sat high on a hill top or made stately journeys from Slieve League to The Roses. As a poet, Allingham had none of the stature of the giant, Yeats, in neighbouring Sligo. He left his native Ballyshannon for London, where he wrote a perceptive and catty diary featuring his literary and artistic acquaintances.

LOUGHROS MORE BAY, COUNTY DONEGAL

When I last visited the bays of Loughros More and Loughros Beg, my daughter was seven years old; we agreed these were the best strands in the world. When the tide goes out over the stripy sand, it reveals caves and leaves big pools of water warmer than the sea, and perfect for a child to swim in. Adults can go surfing, or find the inland lake which has trout, or search out the cromlech said to be one of Diarmuid and Gráinne's beds.

KILLYLEAGH CASTLE, COUNTY DOWN

Although Killyleagh is a seventeenth-century 'Plantation Castle', one of its round corner towers survives from a Norman castle built by John de Courcy in the twelfth century. The towers' pointed roofs were added around 1850, giving the building a romantic outline and the appearance of a Loire chateau. At the top left-hand side of the picture can be seen the great bawn, constructed by Henry Hamilton, the 2nd Earl of Clanbrassil, in around 1666. Its original battlements and gun-holes survive. Later the Earl was poisoned by his wife, after she persuaded him to leave Killyleagh to her instead of to the rightful heirs.

DOWNPATRICK CATHEDRAL, COUNTY DOWN (FAR RIGHT)

St Patrick's Protestant cathedral stands on a hillfort with a view looking down to the Mourne Mountains. The saint himself is reputed to have built a church here in the sixth century. Later he was supposed to be buried at Downpatrick, together with St Brigid and St Columba. The present cathedral was built in the early nineteenth century when the ruins of the earlier monastery on the site were cleared away.

HILLSBOROUGH FORT AND CHURCH, COUNTY DOWN

The town of Hillsborough was founded by the Hill family. The fort was built in the 1650s by Arthur Hill to command the road between Dublin and Belfast. A century later it was rebuilt in the Gothic style with ogee-headed windows. The church of St Malachi, completed in 1772, has a fine Gothic interior, its long nave topped with a ribbed and vaulted ceiling. The Hill family pew is elevated so that the Hills could look down on the congregation.

STRANGFORD VILLAGE AND LOUGH, COUNTY DOWN

Strangford Lough, which is about 12 miles long, is almost landlocked. The strong tide that rushes through the Narrows, visible here beside the pretty village, caused the Vikings to name it Strang Fiord. They founded a base from which to set out on raids along the coast. The site was always strategically important, and Strangford is guarded by four castles.

**KILLYLEAGH,
COUNTY DOWN**

Killyleagh is a little plantation town beautifully sited at the western arm of Strangford Lough. Sir Hans Sloane, whose collection of antiquities formed the basis of the British Museum, was born here in 1666. At the back of the town are the extravagant turrets and pointed roofs of Killyleagh Castle.

**COPELAND ISLANDS,
COUNTY DOWN**

The Copelands, flat as saucers, covered with sheep-nibbled grass and rabbit trails, lie at the entrance to Belfast Lough. Years ago, I flew over them in a microlight, getting a similar view to that photographed by Jason Hawkes. Others may make day trips from Bangor and Donaghadee at the head of Belfast Lough. There is a bird observatory on Lighthouse Island.

**BELFAST CITY
CENTRE,
COUNTY ANTRIM**
You are looking up Royal
Avenue and Donegal Place
towards Donegal Square and
the City Hall. At the
crossroads is Castle Street and
Castle Place. This area was a
controlled zone through the
years of the Troubles, where
there was no access for
vehicles except for buses and
authorized deliveries.
Pedestrians and shoppers had
their bags searched. It would
be good if those terrible times
were over.

BELFAST CITY HALL, COUNTY ANTRIM

For many television viewers, Belfast City Hall is familiar mainly as the background for the banner reading 'ULSTER SAYS NO'. This grandiose building, designed in Renaissance style, its great dome balanced by four little towers in Portland stone, is an Edwardian creation – built at a time when the city fathers were confident in shipbuilding and linen enterprises. The architect was Brumwell Thomas. Inside there is a good deal of Italian marble and stained glass. Monuments in the grounds include a plinth commemorating the arrival of the American Services during the Second World War and, not unsurprisingly, a massive statue of Queen Victoria.

HARLAND AND WOLFF SHIPYARDS, BELFAST, COUNTY ANTRIM

In 1862 a Scarborough-born engineer named Edward Harland went into partnership with C. W. Wolff to found the biggest shipbuilding firm in the world. The great yards of Harland and Wolff are located around the area where the mouth of the River Lagan meets Belfast Lough and on Queen Island.

By 1914 the firm was Belfast's biggest employer with 12,000 men on its payroll. In the past Harland and Wolff built many great ships like the *Adriatic,* the *President Lincoln* and the *Oceanic.* It is a pity that the best known of them is *The Titanic.*

LOOKING EAST FROM LOUGH NEAGH, COUNTY ANTRIM

Lough Neagh, best known for its eels, is the largest lake in either Ireland or Great Britain, its waters, fed by the Upper Bann, supplying much of the needs of the Belfast area. It is relatively unvisited, because the flat and rolling countryside is considered uninteresting. This stretch of farmland, east of the Lough, stretching towards the Irish Sea looks pleasant enough. There is a legend that Lough Neagh was once a fountain that overflowed, drowning whole towns. Thomas Moore wrote how:

On Lough Neagh's banks,
*   as the fisherman strays,*
When the clear cold eve's
*   declining,*
He sees the Round Towers of
*   other days,*
In the wave beneath him
*   shining.*

GLENARM HARBOUR, COUNTY ANTRIM

The village of Glenarm is situated on the south bank of the Glenarm River at the foot of one of the nine narrow valleys known as the Glens of Antrim. Across the river is the wooded demesne of Glenarm Castle, seat of the family of MacDonnell, Earls of Antrim. According to *Murray's Handbook of Ireland*, published in 1878, 'the castle is a modernized and singular mixture of towers, parapets and pinnacles, though the exquisite situation and scenery are sufficient compensation for any architectural inconsistencies'.

DUNLUCE CASTLE, COUNTY ANTRIM
Dunluce Castle, an almost impregnable fortress on top of an island of basaltic rock, was a stronghold of the MacDonnells, Scots freebooters who crossed over to northern Ireland from Caledonian shores. William Thackeray mused on 'those grey towers of Dunluce . . . looking as if some old old princess of old old fairy times were dragon guarded within'. You can peer a hundred feet down a latrine into the turbulent ocean. The servants quarters collapsed into the sea in 1639, together with a number of shrieking servants.

MACAULEY'S HEAD AND BROKEN HARBOUR WALL (FAR RIGHT), GLENARM, COUNTY ANTRIM
The camera captures dour patterns, natural and manmade, along the Antrim coastline.

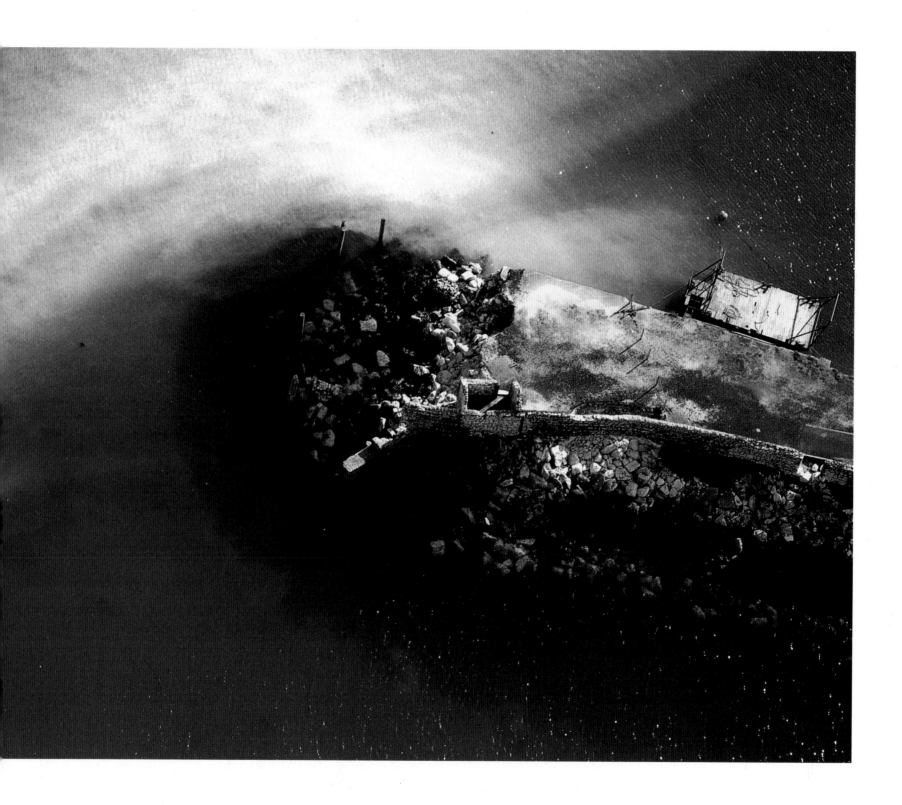

FAIR HEAD CLIFFS AND GARRON POINT (FAR LEFT), COUNTY ANTRIM

In Tertiary times, over 100 million years ago, basalt poured out in a series of flows, faulted and warped into plateaus. The basalts rest on Triassic, Liassic and Cretaceus strata, which are exposed in the escarpments. The remarkable wall-like cliffs of north-east Antrim are the result of these ancient earth movements.

Fair Head, *An Bhinn Mhor,* (the Big Peak) rises 636 feet above huge columns of basalt, which slope away to deep water. There are magnificent views from the Head to Rathlin Island beside the Sea of Moyle where the Children of Lir lived for the second part of their enchantment into swans. On top of the head are three small loughs, one of which is the site of an ancient crannog or Neolithic lake dwelling – an austere and lonely place to have a home.

CARRICK-A-REDE ROPE BRIDGE, BALLINTOY, COUNTY ANTRIM

The swaying rope bridge at Ballintoy over a terrifying 60-foot-wide chasm links the mainland with a great rock stack of black basalt. The bridge helps fishermen laying salmon nets. During the months of winter, storms make the bridge unsafe and it is removed

GIANT'S CAUSEWAY, COUNTY ANTRIM

For many years the Giant's Causeway was difficult to reach. Dr Johnson considered it 'worth seeing, yes; but not worth going to see'. After the building of the coast road between Larne and Portrush, visitors flocked to this wonder of the world. It became as popular a tourist attraction as Killarney. The guides were terrifying; one visitor, Johannes Kohl commented that 'they hunted me as dogs would a deer'. Not every visitor was satisfied. John Gamble felt that 'the sublimity of nature is in irregularity, and she seems downgraded when she counterfeits the trimness of art'.

GRAND CAUSEWAY, COUNTY ANTRIM

There are three main sections of the Giant's Causeway: the Little Causeway, the Middle or Honeycomb Causeway and the Grand Causeway. The actual pavement of over 30,000 even exact columns a foot and a half across, sticks out like a tongue into the sea. This was built by Finn MacCoul so that the Scottish giant, Benandonner, would not get his feet wet before they began their fight.

MIDDLE CAUSEWAY, COUNTY ANTRIM

At the Giant's Causeway, Antrim's basalts are at their most spectacular, with a lower layer of regular, perfectly shaped, hexagonal columns and an upper layer of thin irregular prisms called by names like 'the Giant's Organ', 'the Amphitheatre', 'the Lady's Fan', 'Lord Antrim's Seat' and so on.

Temple of Mussenden, County Londonderry

The Temple of Mussenden was erected by the eighteenth-century Bishop of Derry, Bishop Harvey, in honour of Mrs Frideswell Mussenden, a 20-year-old girl he admired, who died before it was completed. The Bishop was known for his liberal views and for his passion for building – his nickname was the 'Edifying Bishop'. He chose to build Downhill Palace – whose ruin can be seen in the background behind the Temple – on this windblown cliff. Although he planted thousands of trees, not one ever grew.

Perched precariously on its cliff with great views out towards some of the western isles of Scotland, the lovely temple is in its way almost as much a marvel as the Giant's Causeway. It is a domed rotunda with columns, linked by carved stone swags, probably the work of an architect named Michael Shanahan. Inside there used to be a library and a chapel which could be used by all Christian denominations, since the Bishop was ecumenical. He was considered extremely eccentric.

AN IRISH READING LIST

....

BEACH, RUSSELL P. O. (editor): *A. A. Touring Guide to Ireland* (Hampshire, 1976).

CRAIG, MAURICE: *The Architecture of Ireland* (London, 1982).

EVANS, E. ESTYN: *Irish Folk Ways* (London, 1957).

FOX, ARTHUR: *Haunts of the Eagle* (London, 1924).

FREEMAN, T. W.: *Ireland* (London, 1950).

HICKEY, D. J. AND DOHERTY, J. E.: *A Dictionary of Irish History, 1800-1980* (Dublin, 1987).

KILLANIN, LORD; DUIGNAN, MICHAEL V. AND HARBISON, PETER (editors)

The Shell Guide to Ireland (Dublin, 1989).

KISSANE, NOEL (editor): *Treasures from the National Library of Ireland* (Dublin, 1994).

MITCHELL, FRANK: *The Irish Landscape* (London, 1976).

Murray's Handbook for Travellers in Ireland, fourth edition (London, 1878).

NEWBY, ERIC AND PETRY, DIANA: *Wonders of Ireland* (London, 1969).

O'BRIEN, JACQUELINE AND GUINNESS, DESMOND: *Great Irish Houses and Castles* (Weidenfeld & Nicolson, 1992).

O'BRIEN, JACQUELINE AND GUINNESS, DESMOND: *Dublin: A Grand Tour* (Weidenfeld & Nicolson, 1994).

O'CONNOR FRANK: *Leinster, Munster and Connacht* (London, 1960).

ROBINSON, TIM: *Stones of Aran* (Dublin, 1990).

SYNGE, J. M.: *The Aran Islands* (Oxford University Press Edition, 1979).

YEATS, W. B.: *Collected Poems* (London, 1966).

INDEX

....

First published in 1997 by
George Weidenfeld & Nicolson Ltd
The Orion Publishing Group
Orion House
5 Upper St Martin's Lane
London WC2H 9EA

A CIP record for this book is available from the British Library.
ISBN 0-297-83474-6

Design: The Design Revolution
Map: Digital Wisdom
Printed and bound in Italy

Front endpaper: The Big Sugarloaf, County Wicklow
Back endpaper: The Rosses, County Donegal
Title page: Killyleagh, County Down

The photographic images in this book may be obtained
through the Weidenfeld & Nicolson Photographic Archive.
Enquiries by telephone (0171) 498 3011 or by fax (0171) 498 0748.
Many other photographs taken from the air by Jason Hawkes are
available from the Jason Hawkes Aerial Collection,
telephone (0171) 486 2800 or fax (01734) 832634.

PHOTOGRAPHER'S ACKNOWLEDGEMENTS

I would like to thank all those at Weidenfeld, especially Anthony Cheetham, Michael
Dover and Caroline Earle, also everybody at Heli Training & Charter in Belfast.

Thanks as always to Tim, and last, but by no means least, to Adele in Madrid,
come home soon. *Jason Hawkes, December 1996*

AUTHOR'S ACKNOWLEDGEMENTS

Sally Shaw-Smith for showing me so much of the west of Ireland over the years
– Mayo in particular.
Thanks to my sister, Catherine Somerville-Large, for her painstaking
confirmation of the location of a number of sites.
My wife, Gillian, gave me her help and support once again.

I am delighted that Giles Gordon and Michael Dover, publisher of illustrated
books at Weidenfeld & Nicolson, have involved me in this exhilarating project.
Caroline Earle has done a superb job as editor.

Peter Somerville-Large, December 1996